The
Hundred Years
War

Alan Lloyd

The Hundred Years War

General Editor:
Ludovic Kennedy

Hart-Davis, MacGibbon London

Granada Publishing Limited
First published in Great Britain 1977 by
Hart-Davis, MacGibbon Ltd
Frogmore, St Albans, Herfordshire AL2 2NF and
3 Upper James Street, London W1R 4BP

Copyright © 1977 by Alan Lloyd

ISBN 0 246 10869 X

Printed in Great Britain by
William Clowes & Sons, Limited
London, Beccles and Colchester

Contents

Acknowledgements

The photographs and illustrations in this book are reproduced by kind permission of the following. The portrait on page 132 by the gracious permission of H.M. the Queen. Those on pages 46, 47, 76 and 93, Crown Copyright by gracious permission of the Controller of H.M. Stationery Office; pages 10, 36–7, 50, 54, 66–7, 83, 88, 90, 98–9, 102, 104–105, 112–13, 118, 128, 137, 144–5, 160, 162 and 167, Trustees of the British Museum; pages 14, 16–17, 40–41, 44–5, 58, 69, 74, 78, 115, 123, 125, 140–41, 146 and 158, Trustees of the British Library; pages ii–iii, 23, 26, 28, 62, 80, 94–5, 152, 156, 164 and 168, Bibliothèque Nationale, Paris; pages 60, 127 and 130, National Portrait Gallery, London; pages 72–3, Bibliothèque Royale, Bruxelles; pages 18 and 134, Giraudon; pages 20 and 24, The Mansell Collection; pages 30–31, Bodleian Library, Oxford; page 12, Photo: Warburg Institute; page 33, The Governing Body of Christ Church, Oxford; page 65, Foto: Rheinisches Bildarchiv Kölnisches Stadtmuseum; page 109, Museo Arqueologico Nacional, Madrid; page 110, Courtauld Institute of Art, by gracious permission of the Duke of Beaufort; and on page 165, Musée Orléans historique et archeologique Lauros-Giraudon. Illustration Research Service provided the pictures. The maps were drawn by Bucken Limited.

Introduction

The Hundred Years War is remembered for three outstanding battles: Crécy, Poitiers and Agincourt. In each the English won spectacular victory against all the odds. For the first time, the military achievement of the English became a byword throughout Europe, an inspiration for British armies down to modern times. As Shakespeare's Henry V proclaimed of Agincourt:

> This story shall the good man teach his son;
> And Crispin Crispian shall ne'er go by,
> From this day to the ending of the world,
> But we in it shall be remembered ...

Yet the Hundred Years War was much more than a series of battles. Indeed, as Alan Lloyd points out, the confrontation of field armies was a rare event. The brunt of the struggle was borne by non-combatants, the countless civilians who paid for the war not only in taxation but in the plunder, destruction and abuse inflicted on them.

In addition came plague, inflation, repressive social legislation. Little wonder that in both England and France there were dramatic revolts among the working people. Politically and economically, the effects of the war had much to do with the making of modern nations. Militarily, developments were profound and radical.

Here, for *The British at War*, Alan Lloyd provides a fascinating insight into the mind and methods of medieval soldiery, details the major actions, examines the leaders. His canvas is a broad one. Among other things, the Hundred Years War saw the decline of feudal cavalry and chivalric attitudes, the rise of patriotic motivation, the tactical development of long-range hand weapons, the first instances of general actions decided by artillery.

What had begun as a duel between knights in 'gold hewen helmes' ended in gunsmoke. It is a compelling chapter of martial history.

Ludovic Kennedy

Chapter 1

Towards the Contest

At Westminster in January 1327, and at Reims in May of the next year, the two lords whose stratagems were to precipitate what historians have called the Hundred Years War – actually, a series of conflicts spanning about 115 years – first ascended their respective thrones. With the struggle still a decade ahead, few theorists would have contemplated an equal match.

Edward Plantagenet – Edward III – of England was fourteen at accession, and in the tutelage of an adulterous mother, the French-born Isabella, and her ambitious associate Roger Mortimer. Mortimer, having conspired with the English baronage to depose Edward II, headed a fractious coalition of nobles, his eye on the main chance. That the young king should exercise more than nominal authority was no part of the magnate's plan.

In France, the death of Charles IV, last in direct line of the house of Capet, led to the succession of his cousin, Philip VI of the Valois branch. Unlike Edward, Philip not only exerted authority but also possessed powerful personal allies. At thirty-five a proven campaigner, he had already enjoyed considerable influence as Count of Valois, Anjou, Maine, Chartres and Alençon.

No less disparate was the prestige of their kingdoms. Philip's, though not so extensive as modern France (it excluded such eastern regions as Provence, Dauphine, Savoie and Franche Compte), was the foremost power in western Christendom. Its renown was unique, its prosperity unrivalled. Paris, the greatest city of the day with perhaps 150,000 inhabitants, could claim the cultural hegemony of Europe. French towns were marked for their wealth; French agriculture supported a dense rural populace.

By comparison, England was humbled in size and affluence. With a population about a third of France's 10–12 millions, it lagged in both urban and agricultural development, its progress arrested by recurrent bouts of anarchy. Internal and border strife, endemic for centuries, was unresolved. Scotland retained a hostile independence. Ireland was largely in defiance of English rule. Edward's accession had itself been the outcome of civil war.

While the island peoples squabbled, France, if not immune to discord, had experienced an unusually tranquil period for more than half a century. Elsewhere, the German empire declined, denied a worthy ruler since Frederick II, and schism plagued the papacy. To many a lesser prince, including England's adolescent king, the regal mantle donned by Philip of Valois must have seemed as enviable as it was awesome.

Opposite Men-at-arms fighting on foot

11

Edward III of England:
effigy in Westminster
Abbey

In one notable sphere, Guienne, the dominions of the two monarchs overlapped, England's sovereigns being hereditary dukes of that great fief in south-west France. For as long as could be remembered the political anachronism whereby the King of England, as Duke of Guienne, was a vassal of the King of France, had made for friction.

Reluctant to recommend the forceful annexation of the duchy to the domain of their masters, French lawyers had nevertheless exerted considerable wiles to diminish the ducal jurisdiction. English kings, for their part, jibbed at honouring their vassalage.

Other factors encouraged confrontation. The dynastic feuds of royal houses, a depressing saga of self-interest and ill-will, were demonstrated in a claim that Edward, and not Philip, should have occupied the French throne. Ardently advanced by Isabella, a daughter of the house of Capet, the contention galvanized no one but was a card in reserve for Philip's enemies.

Strategically, both kingdoms indulged in flanking policies. While France traditionally supported the Scots in their resistance to English rule, England looked for Rhenish and Low Countries alliances, identifying with industrial Flanders in its quarrels with the French crown. Resenting the authority of the Counts of Flanders and their French suzerains, the rebellious artisans of the Flemish communes had involved the Capetian monarchs in lengthy punitive campaigns which England, a major exporter to the rebel towns, viewed with disfavour.

Amid these and other fluctuating tensions, Guienne remained a singularly constant provocation. Alone of Philip's vassals, Edward, as duke of that region, had failed to do homage to the French king. For some months after his accession Philip was preoccupied with revolt in Flanders, but having suppressed the rebels with ominous thoroughness Philip addressed himself to London. Failing Edward's appearance to take the oath of fealty, Philip would confiscate Guienne 'by force and right'.

There was no avoiding the distasteful chore. Short of war, which the fragile English government dared not risk, appeasement was the only course. In accordance with his councillors, Edward wrote to Philip in April 1329:

My most serene lord and prince, to whom I wish every success and happiness, I would inform your magnificence that I have long desired to visit you and fulfil my duties fittingly; but, due to problems which, as you must know, beset me in my kingdom, I have so far been unable to do so. As soon as I am free, God willing, I shall come to pay the homage I owe you.

13

At Amiens, in June, Edward made good his word. The surround-
ings were not strange to him. Intimate with the rulers of France
through intermarriage, not only were the Plantagenets peers of
that kingdom but they also presided over an English court still
coloured by French culture and language. Edward had lived in
France with his mother at one period. Now seventeen, he returned,
it may be assumed, with an arresting measure of that charm he
was to turn to such good service in later life.

Lithe, sportive and sociable, the embodiment of those knightly
manners which passed for accomplishment in the courts of Europe,
Edward was well able to shine amid the chivalry of France and at
the feasts and tourneys arranged for him. At the oath-taking
ceremony itself, he behaved graciously.

'Sire,' intoned Philip's chamberlain solemnly, 'do you become
the King of France's man for the duchy of Guienne and its
appurtenances?'

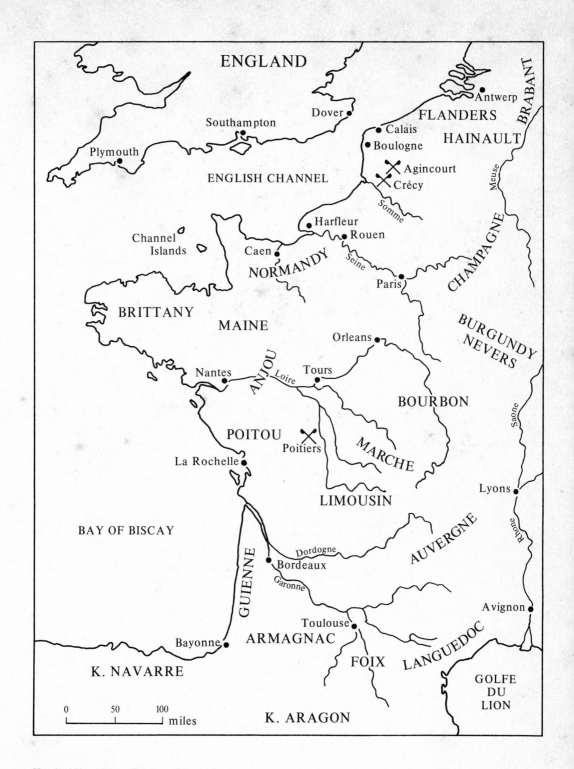

ENGLAND

BRABANT

Antwerp

Dover

FLANDERS

Calais

HAINAULT

Boulogne

Southampton

Agincourt

Crécy

Meuse

Plymouth

ENGLISH CHANNEL

Somme

Harfleur

Rouen

CHAMPAGNE

Channel
Islands

Caen

Seine

NORMANDY

Paris

BRITTANY

MAINE

BURGUNDY
NEVERS

Orleans

ANJOU

Loire

Tours

Nantes

Saône

BOURBON

POITOU

Poitiers

MARCHE

La Rochelle

LIMOUSIN

Lyons

BAY OF BISCAY

AUVERGNE

Rhône

GUIENNE

Dordogne

Bordeaux

Garonne

Avignon

Toulouse

Bayonne

ARMAGNAC

LANGUEDOC

K. NAVARRE

FOIX

GOLFE
DU
LION

0   50   100
miles

K. ARAGON

Edward replied affirmatively, touching his lord's hands.

Notwithstanding the cynicism with which medieval politicians tended to renege their vows, it was a gesture of weighty public and moral significance. Pliant to the will of Philip, no less than to that of Roger Mortimer, the young king can hardly have struck observers as a strong ruler. Judgement was premature. If little in Edward's career was to indicate constancy of policy, let alone statesmanship, far from negligible qualities stirred in him. Complacency was misplaced, as Philip – but more immediately, Mortimer – would learn.

Edward III pays
homage to Philip VI

In England Mortimer's shameless dedication to private gain
was sealing his disrepute. Allies dwindled as his greed increased.
This was Edward's chance to end his dependence on Mortimer,
and he grasped it with an aplomb which foretold his opportunistic
genius. Darkly, on an October night in 1330, sixteen months after
Amiens, he entered Nottingham Castle through an underground
passage and seized the magnate, whose execution at Tyburn
quickly followed. Edward was now his own man.

From the first his inclinations, less for legislature than for war
and diplomacy, struck a chord of neglected harmony in the 17

nation's halls. Contrasting favourably with Mortimer's self-interest, the sovereign's zeal for restoring the prestige of his kingdom appealed to the nobility. In projects of conquest, if in anything, the turbulent barons could find common cause, and a tempting objective was close to hand.

In Scotland, clinging stubbornly to independence despite the efforts of the earlier Edwards, the death of Robert Bruce had left a child, his son David, to face the threat of an Anglophile pretender, Edward Baliol. The little kingdom seemed ripe for plucking. Edward Plantagenet made his plans.

Meanwhile, the humiliating homage to Philip had left a number of unsettled disputes concerning Guienne and its frontiers. Friction between the duke and his suzerain continued. Under renewed French pressure, Edward temporized. His officials in Guienne were instructed to endure provocation 'with good humour and fair words'. Placating missives and ambassadors arrived at the French court from England.

In 1331 Edward returned to France in person to profess his desire for agreement. Marriage between the royal houses was mooted, and Edward, having prudently ingratiated himself with Pope John XXII, proposed an Anglo–French crusade with Philip in high command. Enthusiastically Philip pursued the idea of a 'holy voyage', only to learn that Edward, far from preparing to take the cross, was riding north with court and government.

In 1333, the English king took the offensive in Scotland, crossing the border to support Edward Baliol. At Halidon Hill, in July, Edward added martial intrepidity to improvisation among his demonstrated aptitudes. The result was a triumph. Soon Edward's campaign had opened Edinburgh and Perth to English garrisons and carried his arms as far as Inverness.

Philip, still bent on crusading, watched irascibly. Departure for the Holy Land demanded an understanding with Edward, but it could not be reached at the expense of a free Scotland whose usefulness at times of Anglo–French conflict was axiomatic to French policy. If he persisted in his conquest, he could expect French aid for David Bruce and reprisals in Guienne.

Opposite Philip VI of France

Neither king aspired to the distraction of general war, but by now relations were badly strained. In 1335 legates of a new pontiff, Benedict XII, coaxed a brief truce in Scotland, hopeful of saving the planned crusade. Had the Scots been stronger it might have been maintained. Instead, scenting definitive victory, Edward prepared a final campaign for 1336, gambling on Philip's reluctance to make good his direst threats.

David II of Scotland

For long, intimidation, bluster and cavil had served the French crown in subduing and humbling England's rulers. While Edward II and Mortimer had presided over anarchy and discontent, such tactics had indeed sufficed. That they might not suffice to restrain the new monarch, to contain the changing mood of his baronage, was a proposition yet unrecognized in Paris, where Edward's conciliatory utterances were mistaken for bleats of fear.

20   To impress the warning over Scotland, Philip now made a show

of force, diverting his crusade fleet from Marseilles to the Channel ports. If this were bluff, it succeeded beyond desire. Aborting his Scottish plans, Edward promptly withdrew from the northern realm and, in the autumn of 1336, returned south. But not, as Philip hoped, with humility. Instead, the English king, denouncing French perfidy in Parliament, demanded and was voted subsidies for war with France.

It would be wrong, in considering Edward's temerity, to equate the military strengths of fourteenth-century England and France too precisely with the size and wealth of the kingdoms. At a time when national sentiment was still a weak force, secondary to feudal bonds and regional loyalties, war did not involve the realm-at-large in any modern sense. Indeed, so long as the fighting was not actually close to them, most people knew little of what was primarily the business of a small and select class.

Armies, even those of great kingdoms, were diminutive, recruited from men of individual, often capricious, fidelities, who would have found patriotism an unconvincing concept.

For a variety of reasons, the King of France, the strongest sovereign in Christendom, was lucky if he could raise an army of 20,000 and could realistically depend on nearer half that number in some campaigns. Theoretically, every vassal owed armed contingents to his suzerain monarch in time of war, but the feudal obligation had dwindled as the years passed. Powerful nobles who might have swelled the army with their fighting knights were no longer bound to provide the crown with more than a fraction of the forces they retained for private purposes.

Further, custom limited the service of knights beyond their own provinces to forty days; that of footmen conscripted under feudal law to three months. To offset the obvious shortcomings of such an army, Philip's Capetian predecessors had drawn increasingly on foreign mercenaries while adopting the expedient of paying their feudal troops to stay in the field for extended periods.

By the beginning of the fourteenth century the French army, while retaining its feudal basis, was a paid force. Responding to incentives of up to twenty sous a day for senior knights, and to the fact that regional tranquillity had deprived many of occupation in private wars, substantial numbers of men-at-arms were ready to sell their services to the king, either individually or as *routiers*: members of mercenary bands known as *routes*.   21

In principle, payment disposed towards a much enlarged army. But, in fact, the war treasury lacked the funds for any such force. Despite the general wealth of the country, tradition held that the king should administer and defend the realm at his own expense: that is, with the income from his own domain and personal revenues. Sizeable as this might be, it was severely stretched by the maintenance of government and unfailingly overreached in time of war.

Taxation, a notion as exceptional as it was repugnant to the medieval world, was accepted only as a last resort, and then was widely opposed or evaded by Frenchmen. Since tax collection was ponderous and could not be authorized until hostilities had broken out, its use to finance recruiting was limited. To their ultimate discomfort, French kings resorted to devaluation of the currency as a short-term answer to the problems of war finance.

Withall, the incongruous fact remained that the leading power in Europe depended, when trumpets sounded, on an army that would have made a meagre audience in a modern football stadium.

In England, things were much the same. Like the French force, the English army was still feudal in structure but now paid. The financial resources of the Plantagenets, modest beside those of the French crown, prefigured an even smaller armed array at most times than that fielded by the Kings of France. Edward I's expeditionary force of 1297 had been less than 9,000 strong, while Edward II's army at Bannockburn, among the largest English formations of the period, had not proved equal to fewer than 10,000 Scotsmen.

Even so, the cost of a summer campaign could account for more than half the king's annual revenue. The situation was exacerbated by the need, in most wars against foreign powers, to provide sea transport for the island force. Feudal service owed by seamen of the Cinque Ports was no longer adequate in this respect, and fleets of ships impressed for the purpose added to the crown's expense.

Tactically, the use of military formations by the leaders of both kingdoms was similar. With cannon still in the throes of invention, and footmen subservient to equestrians, cavalry remained the pre-eminent feature of the medieval army, the charge of armoured knights on horseback the dominant battle ploy. Among the factors contributing to this state of affairs could be counted: firstly, the territorial growth of empires, necessitating swift deployments between distant trouble spots; secondly, an emphasis on raiding campaigns rather than pitched battles (itself a result of economic limitations, plus the comparative invulnerability of fortified

Pope Benedict XII

places of refuge); and, thirdly, the development of knightly prowess as a cardinal virtue.

Such élite companionships as the Star, the Garter and the Golden Fleece comprised knights as admired for their horsemanship as for their valour and skill at arms. The horse was indispensable to dignity and high esteem. It raised the nobility above the common crowd, saved the strength of knights on long marches, and allowed their protection by armour of a weight that would otherwise have been insupportable.

Sturdy chargers, or destriers, were prized animals. Kings and princes maintained their own studs, and the breeding and husbandry of war horses, surrounded by innumerable instructions, was less a trade than an esoteric art. While foot followers were regarded as expendable, war leaders were obliged to indemnify their knights against the loss of mounts on active service.

The fraternity of the horseman exceeded politics and frontiers. For the chivalry of Christendom, the brotherhood of crusading enterprise, combat within its own ranks was to some extent governed by gentlemanly conventions which did not extend to mere footmen, the riff-raff of the feudal host. A fourteenth-century chronicler could write that 'the King of England was exasperated' when a number of his humble followers, armed with knives, pushed through his men-at-arms and attacked the enemy knights, 'killing many'. Such behaviour affronted mounted gentlemen on both sides, not least because the capture and ransom of knightly opponents was a lucrative perquisite of war service.

This reliance on equestrian nobility was especially marked in France, the home of chivalry, where squads of well accoutred and practised knights contrasted vividly with the ill equipped and untrained foot levies of town and peasantry. Admittedly, foreign mercenaries had demonstrated the utility of seasoned infantry in some conflicts, but the high fees they demanded, and the abuse they inflicted on a 'friendly' populace, discouraged their use in large numbers.

In England the inferior rating of foot soldiers was tempered with the grudging respect of some commanders. English tradition harked back to an age when the élite had of choice fought dismounted. Harold Godwinson's professional bodyguard, the housecarls, had ridden to battle but fought on foot. Though overthrown by the Normans, they had so impressed their adversaries at Hastings that Anglo–Norman knights had dismounted for every great battle they fought through most of the next century.

Again, recurrent hostilities during the twelfth and thirteenth centuries with the pedestrian but nimble hillsmen of Wales and Scotland had taught English commanders not to despise bowmen and spearmen, particularly when fighting on rough terrain.

An English victory at Falkirk, and later the Scottish triumph at Bannockburn, had provided lessons for those not too hidebound to face the facts. At Falkirk, close formations of Scottish pikemen had repulsed the mounted knights of Edward I's army with significant success until weakened by the arrows of English archers. At Bannockburn, with the ground in their favour, the Scottish 25

26   Paris in the fifteenth century

infantry had advanced quickly to rout the chivalry of Edward II, whose bowmen had been thwarted by a flanking move.

Interestingly, Edward III's first martial achievement at Halidon had been gained in close imitation of the Scottish style. Foot formations, including dismounted knights, had taken the brunt of the fighting, the conventional cavalry charge withheld until the Scots were disorganized. Though the tactics were doubtless attributable to Edward's northern allies under Baliol, the young English sovereign cannot have been unimpressed.

At all events, while cavalry remained the mainstay of English arms, infantry, especially archers, was less disdained in England than it was in France. Comparative rates of pay underlined the fact. A French foot sergeant received a mere twentieth of the remuneration of a French knight, but his equivalent in England could earn a quarter as much as an English knight. The best English archers were rewarded in like ratio.

Finally, so far as war on the Continent was concerned, the King of England could rely on reinforcements from Guienne, the home of redoubtable fighting men. Altogether, the exceptional prestige of France was not entirely reflected in its military organization. Against that kingdom's greater economic resources and consequent capacity for enduring war had to be placed the more compact and coherent martial body of its island neighbour – always provided the violent political passions of England's captains could be directed other than against their sovereign.

Chapter 2

Alliances and Sluys

Edward prepared for war against France with characteristic zeal and ingenuity. Militarily, some of his measures were models for posterity. His commissions of array, regular recruiting boards in the counties to select the fittest men for the infantry, seem remarkably familiar six centuries later. And his insistence on physical exercise, and on target practice to improve archery standards, were notable examples of a new appreciation of the functions of foot troops.

Men-at-arms did not escape his scrutiny. Though himself a tourney enthusiast, Edward banned the sport in the crisis, preferring his knights to concentrate their resources on real conflict. For those unable to speak French, he advised a study of the enemy's language, a refinement surpassing the requirements of later and more sophisticated commanders. If his forces could not match the French in numbers, Edward looked for superior qualities.

Armaments were renewed and overhauled. With the money saved by proscribing expensive tourneys, nobles could make good the loss and damage of equipment in the recent Scottish campaigns. Knightly armour of the period, a combination of plate, mail, leather and quilted fabric, demanded the attention of craftsmen of varied skills.

Linen armourers supplied gambesons and pourpoints, the leather or fabric defences worn respectively beneath and above the mail. Heaumers dealt with helmets. Specialist smiths wrought the items of plate increasingly fashionable not only in the protection of knights but also of their horses, while embroiderers completed the splendid jupens or surcoats which topped the whole panoply:

> ... wrought so weel
> Of goldsmithrie, of browding and of steel;
> The sheeldes brighte, testers and trappures;
> Gold-hewen helmes, hauberks and cote-armures; ...

With the French challenge beckoning, England's armourers worked vigorously to maintain their patrons in that state of martial magnificence evoked by Chaucer's verse. At the same time, bowyers and fletchers were contracted to provide stocks of bows and arrows. The arrows, supplied in sheaves of two dozen, came with or without their forged heads, which were often stored separately. Thousands of bowstrings were ordered, and geese were plucked for the wing feathers which made the arrows fly.

Through the sheriffs responsible for the counties' production of infantry weapons, the arms were delivered to the Tower of London,

Opposite The Battle of Sluys

29

the main national arsenal. It was not a swift process. The demand
for arrows alone (upwards of 240,000 were ordered at a time for
Edward's expeditions) involved a complexity of manual operations,
starting with felling the trees themselves, which severely tested an
industry geared to modest sales. Consignments were commonly
months late.

Greater problems delayed the English king's martial plans.
Already embarrassed by the cost of the Scottish war, Edward
embarked on diplomatic manoeuvres against Philip whose
success was costing him even more. Envoys dispatched through the
Low Countries and the Rhineland to establish an anti-French
coalition to the east of France were empowered to buy alliances
with borrowed cash.

Among others, the Duke of Gelderland and the Counts of
Hainault, Berg, Limburg, Marck, Cleves and Juliers joined the
league, but this cost a great deal. Brabant, the important duchy to
the north-east of Philip, was won over by commercial privileges
which involved diverting English wool from its regular Flemish
30   markets to the young cloth industries at Brussels and Malines.

This move, binding Brabant's prosperity to English friendship while denying Philip's vassal the Count of Flanders the raw stuff of his industrial economy, was politically shrewd but financially upsetting.

Upheaval of the foreign markets disorganized England's wool revenues, which were further confused by Edward's bid for a quick profit by offering a large quantity of requisitioned wool on the Continent. With the treasury empty, trade becalmed, and his taxpayers drained of liquidity, Edward, postponing a contemplated invasion of France in 1337, was obliged to prevaricate during the first half of 1338 at the pope's mediation.

Meanwhile, in negotiations with the impecunious German emperor, Ludwig of Bavaria, Edward careered unhesitantly down the dual trails of diplomatic brilliance and financial recklessness by purchasing the title of Deputy of the Empire. The investiture took place at Coblenz in September before the electors. Amid a splurge of pompous ceremonial, Ludwig pledged himself to a seven-year alliance and bound his princes to serve the new deputy against the King of France.

Smiths and armourers at work, showing (from right) anvil, furnace with bellows and beating armour

31

Edward's prestige soared. Grandly, he added the German eagle to his emblems, struck coins to mark the triumph, and summoned his Continental vassals to do homage. Extravagant festivities suitably dazzled his new allies. To pay for it all, he increased his debt, borrowing deeply from Low Countries and Italian bankers against another wool deal. When the deal failed he pawned his crown jewels.

In France, Philip had his own money problems. Quick to order the seizure of Guienne in response to Edward's intransigence, the French king struggled slowly to military readiness. Efforts to levy a war subsidy from his subjects met the usual opposition and evasions. Vassals claimed that their personal service to the sovereign exempted their followers from taxation. Others insisted on methods of imposition which let them off lightly. Some communities bought their exemption. Normandy obtained release on the promise of maintaining 1,000 men in the field for ten weeks – a quarter of the number looked for in the province.

While his tax collectors haggled and reduced demands, Philip found himself in the invidious position of choosing between military and administrative efficiency. The subsidy produced money so slowly that in 1337 the crown was unable to pay its officials. Salaries had to be cut, and in some cases withheld for twelve months.

In the area of diplomacy, Philip made less ground than Edward. He bought the alliance of the Count of Zweibrücken (Henry of Bavaria), the Bishop of Liège, and the town of Cambrai. He could also depend on the Count of Flanders, and on Luxemburg. Beside Edward's grand coalition, Philip's scattered counter-alliances lacked weight and lustre. But the French king did achieve one coup. By a treaty with Alfonso XI of Castile, he circumvented the possibility of encirclement by his enemies and gained the support of a sizeable Spanish fleet.

Considering the problems facing both sides in their war preparations, it was hardly surprising that the first stages of the conflict were desultory. Philip's troops assumed siege stations at several forts on the frontier of Guienne. A Norman fleet attacked Jersey. French squadrons raided Southampton, Portsmouth, the Isle of Wight and Hastings.

In May 1338 Edward shipped the nucleus of an expeditionary force from Orwell to Antwerp, reinforcing it with further shipments as the months passed in anticipation of an Anglo–Imperial offensive against north-east France in 1339. It was not high on the priorities of his allies. Marking time around Brussels, the English sovereign

waited vainly until September for contingents promised by the Edward III and knights German princes, then, the campaign season almost over, made a brief demonstration on the border.

Though Cambrai was occupied and Thiérache ravaged, Philip refused to be drawn into battle. The approach of winter drove Edward back to Brabant, his manoeuvres having proved little more than a vigorous exercise for his troops and the large pack of hounds he took to war with him.

A less sanguine leader must have wavered. Two years of pre-paration, relentless diplomacy and rash expense had produced a futile foray in which his princely allies had become as conspicuous for their absence as for their cupidity. But if the results counselled caution, Edward ignored them. Still set on sweeping triumphs and a quick verdict, he lavished more borrowed money and concessions on a new friend.

James van Artevelde was an old enemy of Philip and his Flemish vassal Louis of Nevers. Industrial Flanders had not forgotten the oppressions of the French king. Reduced to unemployment and poverty by the diversion of English wool to Brabant, Flemish arti-sans once more turned their resentment against an ostentatiously

33

wealthy count, an affluent nobility, and the meddling officials of Philip's France. Demonstrations supporting 'work and liberty' led to riots and incipient rebellion, developments encouraged by English agents.

In 1338, while Edward was cultivating Ludwig and Brabant, Artevelde, a revolutionary of somewhat incongruous personal wealth, established himself as president of a union of Flemish malcontents, repulsed attacks on Ghent and Bruges by the count's troops, and left Louis no recourse but to flee to the court of France. By early 1339 Artevelde controlled Flanders. An alliance with Edward seemed the logical next step.

Flanders needed the return of English wool for its looms, and mounted men to strengthen its communal foot militia in the advent of a French attempt to reinstate the exiled count. Edward wanted Flanders as a bridgehead to northern France, and coveted the services of the redoubtable Flemish militiamen. For many months Artevelde wrangled over terms before accommodating the English monarch at a high price.

In December 1339, on the morrow of the abortive Thiérache campaign, an agreement was concluded by which Edward granted the Flemings free access to English wool, the promise of military aid in case of French attack, and substantial sums of money (payable in four instalments) to be spent improving the defences of Flanders. In return, Artevelde pledged military support for Edward's campaigns and recognized his revived claim to the crown of France, conveniently disposing of any Flemish qualms over feudal obligations to Philip.

On the face of it, Edward had scored again. Still in his twenties, he might be heavily in debt, attended as closely by creditors as by courtiers, but his titles glittered beyond gold, not least in his own eyes. Self-styled 'King of England and France', deputy of the German empire, he sat in state at Ghent receiving the homage of Philip's enemies.

It was only when he wished to sail to England for reinforcements that reality intruded. Embarrassingly, he was obliged to leave his wife Philippa, daughter of the Count of Hainault, and their young children, as hostages to Dutch bankers against his agreed return in four months.

Back at home Edward found the Commons in revolt over repeated sacrifices for a war which had produced no results, and an administration sick of control from the Continent. Further military and taxation projects were hindered by general disgruntlement. 34 Worse, Philip, determined to prevent Edward's reappearance in

Flanders with fresh arms, stationed the French fleet, powerfully reinforced by Castilian squadrons, off the Flemish coast in the spring of 1340.

The first major engagement of the Hundred Years War was to be at sea. On the result would hinge the credibility of Edward's Continental ambitions.

Fourteenth-century fleets were for the most part conglomerates of commercial vessels and their crews impressed to special service at the king's command. Even in times of peace, merchant ships might be 'arrested' to transport crown officials and property overseas. During wars, such measures were employed extensively, admirals being appointed with disciplinary powers over men on fleet service.

Traditionally, two admirals supervised England's war fleets, one responsible for ports 'from the Thames northward', the other for ports 'from the Thames westward'. The vessels at their disposal, mostly designed for coastal trade or short hauls across the Channel or Irish Sea, varied in displacement from as little as fifty tons to approaching 200 tons, the majority not exceeding 100 tons.

With a single mast, a large square sail and such comparatively recent innovations as stern rudders and bowsprits, these beamy little craft fell broadly in three naval categories: first, unmodified merchant ships; second, merchant ships 'fitted for the king's service'; and, third, 'the king's ships'.

The second category comprised vessels adapted for warfare by the fitting of raised decks and mast stations from which missiles could be rained on an enemy. The third and least numerous group, built expressly as warships, sported regular castles fore and aft, and shielded crow's-nests. Usually large by prevailing standards, they formed the fighting pride of the royal navy, the nucleus of the battle fleet.

Overleaf The Council of the King of France and ships of Sluys

Eminent men lived well aboard these ships. Of a nobleman who embarked from Scotland in 1338, it was said that 'he kept an honourable table all the while, with trumpets and drums ... his plate was gold and silver, with pots, basins, porringers, goblets, bottles, barrels, etc. Moreover, he had twenty-six young and gentle squires to wait on him.'

The crews themselves, remarkably large for the size of the ships involved (some carried a hundred and more mariners), were less refined. Admiralty instructions included a scale of fines by which

captains might hope to keep peace aboard. A sailor who accused his shipmates of lying should be made to pay four pence; if he lied to the master, eight pence; if he hit the master, five shillings. And, 'If the master smite any of the mariners, the mariner ought to abide the first buffet be it with fist or flat of hand, but if smitten more times the mariner may defend himself.'

Other offensive acts were penalized by ducking and keel-hauling. The fishermen, part-time pirates and others who sailed their small craft to Orwell in the summer of 1340, ready to carry Edward and his new recruits to Flanders in defiance of Philip's fleet, were a tough lot. Many of them thought nothing of plundering the ports and vessels of their fellow countrymen in slack periods.

According to the chronicler Robert Avesbury, Edward challenged those of his seamen who were afraid of the French navy to 'stay at home'. It was an invitation he could make with assurance of a poor response.

Passing Whitsun at Ipswich, the king sailed from Orwell on 22 June with approximately 200 ships, being joined at sea by his northern admiral, Sir Robert Morley, with fifty more. Geoffrey le Baker of Swinbrook, another chronicler, put the entire fleet, 'great and small', at 260 craft. Some were transports carrying, among other cargoes, horses for the men-at-arms. One conveyed the queen's household, bound from England to attend Philippa on the Continent.

Next day, Edward anchored at Blankenberghe, north of Bruges, where he put down three squires to reconnoitre the enemy blockade. The French and Spanish fleet, accompanied by a number of Genoese galleys serving as mercenaries, was stationed before the town of Sluys, or Sluis, on a broad inlet (since silted up by the River Eede) used by shipping for Bruges and inland Flanders. English historians later claimed that the enemy outnumbered Edward in vessels, but Edward himself wrote of 190 hostile sail.

Since the ships themselves carried scant offensive armament, the number of men available for boarding actions was more relevant than a count of masts. On this score, the English fleet, packed with fresh troops for Flanders, was well served.

Their opponents, under the high command of Nicholas Béhuchet, a former treasurer for the French king, included the admiral Hue Quiéret of France, and the Genoese professional Barbavera, an astute captain who viewed the confrontation with some doubts. While Barbavera favoured putting to sea to meet the English, Béhuchet, intent on blocking the road to Bruges, declined to leave the anchorage. His choice of a defensive station left him open to the possibility of small-boat intervention by the Flemings on the near shore.

Béhuchet arrayed his fleet in several lines, the ships chained together to prevent penetration and dispersal by the enemy. The technique was an ancient one. Three centuries earlier, Harald Hardrada and Sweyn Estrithson had lashed their ships into giant rafts to fight at Nisaa. The tradition of regarding fleets as floating battlefields on which troops emulated land conflicts was still strong. It demanded the calm water of sheltered bays and estuaries.

On the morning of 24 June, the feast of St John the Baptist, Edward led his force into the roadstead. He was in the cog *Thomas*. Behind, decks thick with swordsmen and archers, streamed his motley armada. Ahead, like the turreted walls of a great fort, stretched the solid lines of the enemy, rocking gently in an easterly breeze. Among the French and Spanish squadrons rode a score or so of the largest ships then seen – a sight, it appears, which impressed many Englishmen. But they had little time to dwell on it. Taking advantage of the conjunction of wind and low sun, Edward attacked immediately. It was about 9 a.m.

Baker's account, doubtless gleaned from eye-witnesses, provides a vivid impression of medieval sea warfare. As the English closed, 'the whole fleet gave a terrible shout, and a shower of arrows from longbows poured down on the Frenchmen'. Skilled marksmen placed on forecastles and in crow's-nests could take a heavy toll of their opponents before the ships touched. 'Eventually they came hand-to-hand with pikes, poleaxes and swords, and some hurled stones from the tops, braining many.'

The battle, a long and bloody succession of boarding actions, raged all day. Seemingly by concentrating on one French formation at a time, the English made headway. The tall Castilian vessels were particularly hard to capture, but the first and second lines of defence had succumbed by dusk. Poor liaison between French and Spaniards, and the distaste of the Genoese for the tactics of Béhuchet, had not helped the Continentals.

Nor, as the day turned against them, did the rigidity of their formations. One consequence of chaining ships together was that it hampered the withdrawal and redeployment of the hard-pressed. Unable to detach their craft in the last resort, 'many Frenchmen abandoned them and leapt overboard'. Darkness, and the exhaustion of the attackers, offered some respite, but it also enabled groups of Flemings to approach from the shore and board French ships.

Edward minimized the role of his allies, perhaps unaware of 39

41

much that occurred in the night, but French accounts of the battle concede its significance. At all events, though a number of Béhuchet's vessels had escaped by dawn, the French fleet had not effectively reorganized. Barbavera opted for discretion. Extricating his squadron, he disappeared on the morning of the 25th.

The remaining French ships fought on until overwhelmed. Béhuchet and Quiéret perished along with hundreds of their men, most of whose vessels were captured by the English. For some, it was a return to old colours. Among others, the *Denis*, the *George*, the *Blacke Cocke* and the *Christopher* (one of the larger vessels of its day) were of English origin, seized earlier by the French on the Flemish coast.

French legend came to assert that Edward was wounded at Sluys in personal combat with Béhuchet. Reliable testimony for such an incident is lacking, but it is not improbable. The English king certainly enhanced his reputation for intrepidity in the battle. It was far from being an easy victory. Indeed, Edward's decision to rest at anchor for several days afterwards is consistent with a stiff enemy defence and the likelihood that the English suffered heavily.

Early reports of the losses are dubious. Baker put the French and Spanish dead at about 25,000, a figure in excess of the total strength of most armies of the period. Yet, allowing for the gross exaggeration of the chroniclers, it is evident that Sluys was a singularly costly clash. While medieval foot troops were seldom shown quarter, the bulk of a worsted army on land could always break and run for it. At sea, only water welcomed the fugitives, few of whom, even among sailors, could swim.

Presaging many years of English naval dominance, the victory at Sluys spared England the fear of depredations and invasion, and also secured Edward's communications with the Continent. Few events could have represented a more auspicious prelude to an Anglo–Flemish offensive against upper France. Yet, that summer it came to nought.

Strategically, the notion of a decisive thrust in the north-east, diverting attention from Guienne and striking Philip in a theatre better suited to Edward and his allies, was sound enough. Unfortunately for Edward, he still lacked the resources for a sustained advance. At Tournai, his first target on the frontier of the royal domain of France, the English king was halted by lack of siege equipment.

Edward was not short of troops. His combined force of English and Flemish contingents numbered upwards of 20,000, an army confident of tackling Philip's on the battlefield. But Philip was too canny to risk a showdown which might result in a second Sluys. Philip has been maligned as indecisive, and slow to act against Edward, but his land campaign of 1340 was immaculate.

Skirting the allies at Tournai, the French army prowled the Flemish frontier from Artois towards Lille, separating the anxious county from that part of its militia that was with Edward. Thus inhibiting the enthusiasm of the Flemings to march farther from Flanders, Philip intensified the war of nerves by falling on outlying allied detachments, harrying foragers, and disrupting the assembly of fodder that Edward would need as the summer closed.

Time was in Philip's favour. To his east, the grand structure of alliances founded on English gold already teetered in the chill wind of Edward's insolvency. Brabant, drawn to England by the diversion of the wool trade from Flanders, defected as exports were restored to the Flemish communes in accordance with Arte-velde's requirements.

Patient, if less spectacular in diplomacy than Edward, the French king now achieved reconciliation with the Count of Hainault, whose double relationship as vassal and brother-in-law of Philip belatedly outweighed his sentiments as father-in-law of the English monarch. Even the Sluys defeat held some profit, for, aroused at last to the imminence of danger, Philip's subjects showed a fresh respect for royal authority. Tax collection signifi-cantly improved.

The full size of Edward's task was emerging, and by mid-September, with the weather breaking and supplies low, he was not sorry to accept a truce, proposed by papal envoys, to last until next summer. For all his grandiose schemes, and his resounding naval victory, the kingdom of France remained inviolate, stronger and more cohesive than ever. Impetuosity, the young English sovereign was learning, did not assure the best results.

Chapter 3

The Path to Crécy

In November 1340, a month after the Truce of Esplechin, Edward slipped secretly from Ghent and fled his creditors to England. Behind, he left mercenaries unpaid and a chain of Continental merchants and bankers faced with ruin. When the Italian banks of Bardi and Peruzzi, which had made him enormous loans, were bankrupted at last by his insolvency, every banking house in Europe felt the repercussions.

Edward's plans were shattered. His expensively purchased coalition was gone. In 1341 Ludwig of Bavaria revoked the deputy-ship of the empire and led his princes into neutrality. Flanders, hit by the collapse of English credit, wavered. Urged by the French court, the pope excommunicated the Flemish rebels for breaking allegiance to their lawful lord. Artevelde had already displeased his working class supporters by increasing his unseemly wealth in office.

Now, as Count Louis began to regain ground, the rebel leader sought desperate remedies. In an attempt to check the count's resurgent authority, Artevelde offered the coronet of Flanders to Edward's eldest son and namesake, the Duke of Cornwall, soon to be Prince of Wales, the so-called Black Prince. The expedient disgusted Flemings of all persuasions. In 1345 Artevelde was murdered by his own townsmen.

Meanwhile, Edward vented his frustration at home by accusing his officials of ignoring his orders from overseas and failing to find the money he needed. In particular, he rounded on his chancellor, Robert Stratford, and on Stratford's brother John, Archbishop of Canterbury. Fearing arrest, the archbishop took sanctuary at the monastery of Christchurch while the bankrupt and humiliated king wreaked indiscriminate vengeance on judges, sheriffs, tax collectors and others.

Such action hardly relieved the economic situation, nor furthered Edward's war aims. Reduced to living on his wits, the king per-suaded a syndicate of English merchants to loan him money against customs revenues, and sought a cheaper road than hitherto to conquest. The year 1341 blessed him with a happy fortuity.

In the first half of the year, the focus switched to Brittany. Here, the death of the duke, John III, tempted his half-brother, John of Montfort, to defy the French monarch by seizing the fief without investiture. Fearful of Philip's anger, John sailed to England to seek Edward's help. It was eagerly granted. With the great western shoulder of France detached from Philip's realm, the whole balance of the war would shift from the east, the scene of

Opposite English troops on the march

45

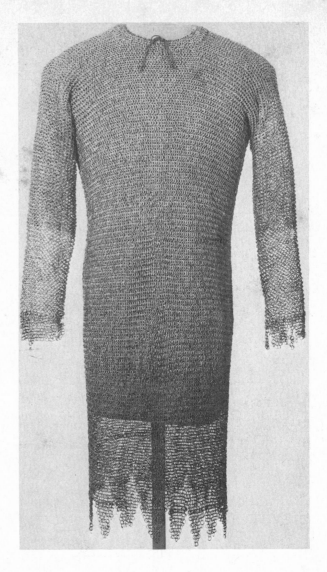

Medieval mail shirt

English failure, to a promise of fresh triumphs.

While John of Montfort pledged homage to Edward, Philip promptly proclaimed his nephew Charles of Blois the new Duke of Brittany, dispatching a force to support his choice. Montfort was captured, but his wife, Joan of Flanders, pursued the fight against Charles of Blois, whose cause was stoutly championed by his own spouse, Joan of Penthièvre.

For the most part, the so-called War of the Two Joans belongs to French internal history, but in 1342 Edward personally intervened with an army, provoking a French counter-incursion led by Duke John of Normandy, Philip's son and heir. Before the two hosts

46

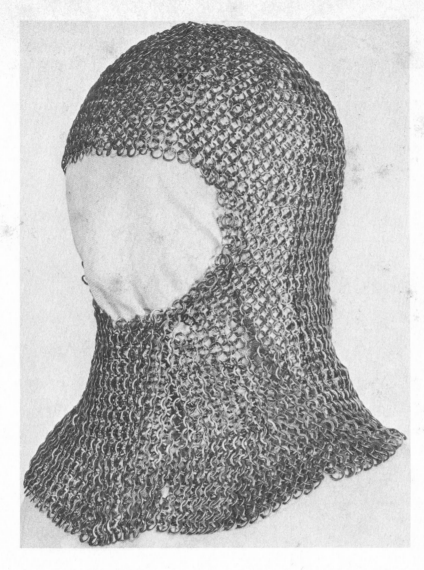

could meet, papal legates imposed a new truce (the Truce of Malestroit, January 1343), robbing the chivalry of the two kingdoms of the pitched battle awaited now for five years.

Extending for three years, the truce did not prevent Edward installing garrisons at strategic points in the duchy, shutting up Joan of Flanders, who had gone mad, and assuming guardianship of her young son. The strength of his hold on Breton affairs was acknowledged tacitly in negotiations under the auspices of Pope Clement VI. The French offered to restore Guienne with widened frontiers as part of a settlement.

Philip was not, however, willing to surrender sovereignty of 47 that fief, the crux of the English king's terms for peace. As the French had failed in practice to occupy Guienne, its 'restitution' less than gratified Edward's quest for sweeping gains. The expiry of the truce in 1345 found him freshly confident. Brittany had provided a valuable interlude. True, Flanders was rife with disaffection, but what price Flanders when Edward had the Breton ports!

Early in the summer of 1346, the lanes of southern England rumbled with wagons, horse-drawn and ox-drawn, bearing supplies to the coast for the first royal expedition since hostilities had recommenced. Knights and their servants rode south by down and forest. Villages echoed the songs of foot soldiers wending their way to the sea from ale-house to ale-house. Many had marched from Wales. Records detail the reluctance of Welsh troops to leave home without a travel allowance in their pockets. Doubtless, it was well spent before they reached port.

Though Wales retained a strong national feeling, the age-old hostility of Celt and Saxon had mellowed by the fourteenth century. Welsh soldiers were a familiar sight in English armies. Some were archers, but their fame was for fighting with long spears, and with the knives they carried as side-arms. With them came bowmen from Cheshire and Flintshire, like the Welshmen clad in uniforms, or *cotecourtepiz*, of green and white.

The provision of official clothing for infantry, while not yet general, was becoming increasingly commonplace. Kings and magnates liked their men to look distinctive. The chamberlain of Chester was instructed to 'deliver each [soldier] a short coat and a hat of both colours, the green on the right'.

Cheshire archers had a high reputation, commanding better pay than others. Long since, the region had excelled in its resistance to the Normans. Constant fighting against the inroads of the Welsh had inured its men to the rigours of warfare. Moreover, it offered special sanctuary for fugitives from justice, desperadoes who welcomed the anonymity and adventure of army life.

The size of Edward's expeditionary force of 1346 cannot be estimated reliably. Intended for a major offensive on its own account – the first of the war in which allied support was not envisaged – most likely it was large by English standards of the time, though that is a modest claim. Even Froissart, as prone to exaggeration as other early chroniclers, put Edward's combatants at less than 20,000. Perhaps 12,000 would be nearer the number.

In addition, a substantial body of non-combatants accompanied the army: servants, carters, farriers, cooks, armourers, and so on. Hundreds of horses were marked for embarkation, plus vehicles needed in the baggage train. Special gangways, or *pontes*, were built for the loading of animals, and hurdles were ordered to separate the closely packed and kicking horses aboard ship. Then there was such freight as tents, pavilions, mills, ovens and forges, not to mention the plate and lavish wardrobes of noblemen, some of whom enshipped their hounds and falcons.

Strict secrecy surrounded the destination of the expedition until it put to sea. The ubiquity of spies and informers at this period is attested by the sound intelligence at rival courts. The conveyance of news, even across seas, was a swifter business than the movement of armies. Brittany, it could scarcely have been doubted, was a likely goal. Contingents under a resourceful captain, Thomas Dagworth, had been extending English interests there since the truce ceased.

On the other hand, Guienne was currently the scene of major action. Here the successes of an Anglo–Gascon army under Henry, Earl of Derby (later Duke of Lancaster), had attracted a formidable French force led by the Duke of Normandy. As Edward assembled his armada, the French prince was besieging Aiguillon, a key stronghold of the Gascon plain. A landing in Guienne was not implausible, and the notion may have been encouraged to deceive spies.

Tuesday 11 July revealed the truth. That morning the English fleet, approaching the north-east point of Cotentin, put in at a sheltered site named Saint Vaast la Hougue. Edward had based his choice of location on the defection to England of a Norman baron, Geoffrey of Harcourt, whose family was influential in Cotentin. With the Brittany garrisons to cover him, the English king could mount his strike with some security.

It would be rash to ascribe conventional military objectives to early raiding warfare. In effect, Edward's campaign both took advantage of the preoccupation of French arms in Guienne, and relieved pressure in that theatre. It would also, as it happened, precipitate the first notable land battle of the war. But that such considerations impelled the offensive is dubious.

An essential aspect of medieval dynastic warfare was the impressing of brutal realities on a rival's subjects. By terrorizing and ravaging their homes, the invader demonstrated the impotence of the incumbent lord to protect his own, thus inducing political 49

50   Pillagers at an armoury

pressure to undermine the enemy. To this extent, war was a glorified protection racket, occasionally involving the confrontation of armies, more often casting the innocent and defenceless as victims.

Since it scarcely mattered whether this village or that town was sacrificed in the exercise, raiding campaigns had an opportunistic bias. Among other factors, the need to victual from the land, the prospects for loot, and the possibilities of encountering pockets of local resistance influenced decisions and dictated the onward path.

The full disembarkation of Edward's expedition took several days, during which detachments sacked nearby Barfleur, attacked Cherbourg and plundered the countryside. A batch of young English bloods, including the Black Prince, then sixteen years of age, was knighted on landing to solemnize the coming role. Finally, on 18 July, the entire army headed for lower Normandy and Caen, the ancient capital.

From a number of accounts, not least those of William Retford, Clerk of the King's Kitchen on the campaign, the march appears to have taken an inconsistent course, now diverting abruptly from the main course, now lingering without apparent purpose, now embarking on an inexplicably brief or long march in an advance which averaged a fairly leisurely five or so miles a day. Such variations, independent of the proximity of any French army, accord with the raiding methods of the day.

Detours to towns rich in booty gratified troops who had enlisted in the expectation of supplementing their pay with loot, and also topped up the royal treasury. Theoretically, church possessions were sacrosanct, but the high value of sacred vessels and altar hangings proved too tempting in some instances. Plundering might delay the advance for a day or two, then buildings were fired and the force moved on.

This policy of inflicting *damnum*, or loss, on a locality was pursued with contempt for its inhabitants. Peasant farmers were stripped of their cattle, hay and corn; food stores were carried off; abusive, uncouth troops entered cottages, ransacked their few treasured possessions and brutalized the occupants. Having feasted at the tables of their victims, the soldiers burned their dwellings.

The approach of the army, signalled by smoke and the glow in the sky at night, filled old and young with panic. Its passage left a trail of bereavement, dislocation and ruin.

If the realities of campaigning mocked the pretensions of chivalry, they seem not to have worried the nobility. The age accepted an ethical dichotomy by which its chroniclers, having declared their 51

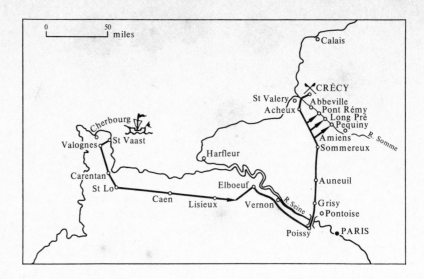

Edward III's March to Crécy

intention of glorifying knightly deeds and virtues, went on to fill their stories with guile, greed and cruelty. Indeed, the contradiction appears to have eluded them.

The fact is that chivalry, though at the height of its outward brilliance, was a hollow code, an elaborate social convention pertaining only to the upper class. From earliest youth, its aspirants were trained to equate formality and etiquette with ideals. Knights would engage in ridiculous contests to see who could be the most polite, then resort from envy to bloodshed. Chivalry had become an heroic illusion, a form of ceremonial display divorced from the duties of daily life, especially of martial life, in which elevated concepts were seldom convenient.

Militarily, chivalry concerned the arts of war and worthy opponents. It was not to loot and vandalize that Edward's knights had learned the skills of jousting and equipped themselves so splendidly. But the arts of war were seldom demanded. The practice of war was largely ungallant work.

Thus ingloriously, Edward progressed through France. In late July he occupied Caen. Having thoroughly pillaged it (he shipped the plunder down the Orne to the English fleet), he proceeded via Lisieux to the Seine above Rousen. For a week, from 7 August, he ravaged the Seine valley. Pont de l'Arche, Vernon, St Germain and St Cloud were burned. At last, almost at Paris, the invaders crossed the river and turned for the coast, heading due north.

Philip's beard had been well scorched. Waiting in the capital for his forces to concentrate, particularly for the return of those deployed in Guienne, the French king had watched Edward's depredations with mounting wrath. A French advance at half-strength, perhaps the move Edward wanted, would have given the English a battle on their terms. Philip preferred to muster the full weight of his superior numbers, hoping his rival might tarry imprudently.

It was a near thing. Intent on slipping away towards Boulogne to rejoin the English fleet, Edward was delayed on the Seine by broken bridges. From Elboeuf to Poissy, the French had destroyed every crossing place, obliging the invaders in the end to stop and effect repairs. By 15 August, when Edward gained the north bank at Poissy, a formidable army was ready to march under Philip. The chase was on.

The French army which issued vengefully from Paris, more than twice the size of the English force, comprised in chief the flower of Philip's chivalry backed by militia from the communes. To compound the numerical disparity, it was reinforced by a contingent of Genoese mercenaries, skilled crossbowmen, and allied divisions under, among others, the Count of Flanders and the veteran King of Bohemia, whose advanced age and blindness did not keep him from his battle horse. The odds against Edward were reflected in his rapid flight.

In three days, after crossing the Seine, the English army covered about fifty miles, from Poissy through Grisy and Auneuil. It was a determined pace for an army laden with booty, which had been on the road for many weeks. All the same, the French matched Edward's forced marches. They were close on his heels as he reached the Somme.

Again, a river checked the English king. This time the bridges were intact, but local forces, emboldened by Philip's proximity, guarded them stubbornly. At Picquigny, Long Pré and Pont Rémy, attempts to cross were thwarted. The retreating army had ranged the south bank almost to the estuary, where it faced being trapped against the marshy flats.

Then, at Boismont, a village approaching the river's mouth, Edward was saved by word of a nearby ford. At low tide, his troops were able to cross 'twelve abreast, the water knee-high'. Even so, the far bank was contested and the English vanguard had to fight 53

The Battle of Crécy

its way ashore. The crossing was timely. As the army scrambled to
the north bank, part of its baggage train, still waiting to cross the
stream, was overwhelmed by Philip's advanced patrols.

Now the tide became Edward's friend. With the water rising,
Philip had to await the next ebb or divert to Abbeville, the nearest
crossing upstream. Allowing for the extended order of the French
force, whose contingents were spread over many miles, Edward
could depend on a breathing space of at least a day before Philip
could come up to him.

54

He had escaped disaster, but the choice before him was not enviable. Either, he could drive his fatigued columns forward and risk being overhauled on unfavourable ground, or he could use the short grace provided by the tide to prepare a stand on some select site.

By Friday 25 August, encamped near the small town of Crécy a few miles beyond the Somme, Edward had decided on the second course. Chivalric tradition, the code affected no less by the English than by the French knights, presumed a more or less neutral battlefield on which the opposed nobility might test its prowess shield to shield, spur to spur. Hopelessly outnumbered in men-at-arms, the English could never have survived in such conditions. If they were to fight with any real chance, it had to be with ingenuity and cunning, rejecting noble pretensions and adopting the pragmatic tactics of Scotland and the Welsh marches. Such were the paradoxes of Crécy that the numerical weakness of Edward's army was to prove its strength; the effacement of knightly glory, its lasting fame.

Edward disposed his troops in three divisions, or battles, on a front of about a mile and a half between Crécy and the neighbouring village of Wadicourt. The right wing covered the former, the left the latter. Two divisions were in the front line, that of the Earls of Northampton and Arundel on the left, that of the Black Prince on the right. A third, under the king himself, formed a second line or reserve ahead of the baggage.

Each division consisted of a central formation of nobles and men-at-arms with extended wings of archers and spearmen, these inclined forward and likened to the points of a 'herse' or harrow.

Several features gave the arrangement subtlety. A marshy stream, the Maye, rising near the village of Fontaine, on the road to Abbeville, and winding back to Crécy, protected the right flank, while steep ground discouraged a flanking move against the left. Confronting Philip's advance from Abbeville, gentle undulations in the terrain disguised the extent of the upward haul to the English line, which occupied the forward slope of an eminence. Equally concealed by the folds was a reedy trough, the so-called Val aux Clercs, draining toward the Maye across Edward's front.

To complete these circumspect, if unsporting, considerations, the English archers and their supporting spearmen were hidden as far as possible by hedge and thicket. While the advancing enemy had a deceptively incomplete view of what lay ahead, Edward occupied a station from which he could observe the French approach clearly for a long way.

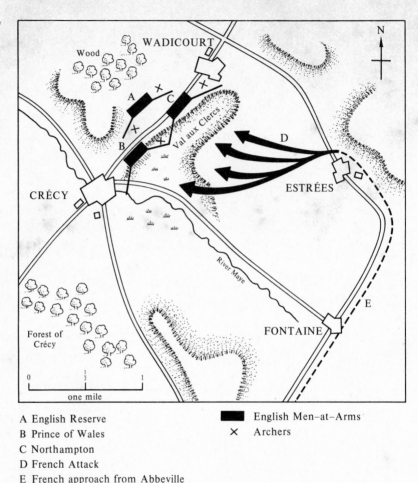

A English Reserve
B Prince of Wales
C Northampton
D French Attack
E French approach from Abbeville

■ English Men–at–Arms
✕ Archers

What he saw was encouraging. In the race to overhaul the quarry, Philip's host had opened into a series of dispersed and straggling contingents separated by many miles. In contrast to the small but cohesive English army, the overwhelming numbers of the enemy were divided not only by independent commands (French, Flemish, Bohemian, etc.) but also by wide differences of martial skill and spirit.

Among the French, there was no first-class infantry. Though the *milice des communes* and peasant levies proliferated in great swarms, they were undisciplined and poorly armed. For generations, kings and nobles had distrusted them, fearing to train and equip them lest they revolt. The chivalry, jealous of its glory, had no wish to share victories with the *ribaudaille*.

Nor were the French knights, resplendent in their mounted cavalcades, conspicuously well controlled. Eager for retribution against the English despoilers, they began to reach the field on the afternoon of Saturday the 26th far ahead of the toiling infantry. Impatiently, they reined their horses around Estrees, a village to the English front.

Philip was not a rash commander. Instinct cautioned him to halt and bivouac, to defer battle until his army had closed up and the field been reconnoitred. But the wilfulness of his knights overruled the plan. Committed to immediate action, he tried to make the best of it. Alone of his footmen, the professional cross-bowmen from Italy had come on in good, if weary, order. Without adequate rest, they were sent forward to soften the English line.

At this crucial moment, Edward had a stroke of luck. A thunderstorm pelted the countryside. Established in position, the English archers contrived to keep their bows dry. The advancing Genoese were less fortunate. The first volley from their dampened crossbows was ineffective.

The response was withering. Expertly handled, the five-foot longbows of the English and Welsh propelled their yard-long shafts with deadly accuracy. An accomplished archer could fire twenty aimed shots a minute, each lethal at 200 yards and more. The crossbowman, with a complicated winding and laying drill, could not match such a rate of fire.

Despondently, the Italians fell back with heavy losses. They were ridden down by the leading French knights, who cursed them for a 'faint-hearted rabble'. The resulting confusion was exacerbated by a further stream of English arrows and a second wave of impetuous cavalry. It was decimated before reaching the English line.

Surging through the soggy hollow of Val aux Clercs, the knights of John of Bohemia were peppered by flying shafts. As stricken mounts tumbled, their unhorsed riders floundered uselessly in heavy armour. Among the few who reached their objective, the blind king, surrounded by a band of loyal lieutenants, was killed attacking the station of the Black Prince.

Furiously, fresh contingents of French knights spurred on their mounts to challenge the English chivalry. Intent on reaching their counterparts, they seem to have ignored the enfilading archers who picked them off greedily. Those attackers who survived the flying shafts found Edward's knights curiously unresponsive to the summons of mounted duel, phlegmatically arrayed in defensive formation like foot troops. Beside them, Welsh spears bristled.

Crécy, battle detail

Tactically, there was little variation in the assaults which, on one authority, were pressed in sixteen distinct waves. Dusk presented no respite. Long after the sun had set on the armour of the French charge, forays continued in the darkened vale. Now, the dead were an obstacle in themselves, hampering Philip's knights, increasing their rage and frustration.

Only after midnight did the English, construing the danger past, venture victoriously forward with lanterns to despatch or capture wounded enemies, to loot and search for dead dignitaries. It was dawn before Edward's heralds, sent to tally the corpses, could quantify the triumph. The total losses of Philip's army are unknown, but 1,542 of his nobility were reported dead. English losses were put at about fifty.

Despite repeated French charges, close pressure on Edward's formations had never been worrying. The familiar story that at one point Edward declined to reinforce the Prince of Wales, saying 'Let the boy win his spurs', suggests nothing more certain than the lack of real crisis. The comparative losses are explicable only by missile preponderancy. Hand-to-hand fighting was minimal.

On 27 August, the morrow of the débâcle, Philip fled in horror from his first defeat, alone except for a few close retainers. Behind him, the pride of France's chivalry, the King of Bohemia, the Count of Flanders and innumerable foreign noblemen lay dead. The greater part of the French infantry, never having set foot on the battlefield, dispersed bemusedly southwards on hearing the astounding news.

Chapter 4

Black Death; Black Prince

Victor against all expectation at Crécy, Edward continued his march to the Channel intent on re-embarkation. As his port he chose Calais, a possession of the county of Boulogne and the nearest point on the French coast to England. What followed elaborates an aspect of fourteenth-century warfare already mentioned: the inefficiency of siege equipment and techniques.

Calais, with strong walls and a rugged populace, defied the English so stubbornly that only Edward's own obduracy prevented his army from giving up. As autumn turned to winter and the port had still not been captured, the high spirits generated by Crécy departed and English desertions began to mount. Winter campaigning was neither expected nor relished. Spring threatened the return of Philip with another host.

Indeed, by the early summer of 1347 Philip had collected a fresh army, though smaller than hitherto, and was advancing toward the beleaguered port. But commander and troops wanted confidence. The trauma of Crécy hovered over them. Philip remembered the incoherence and wilfulness of his force. Its survivors recalled his failure to impose control.

The attempt to intervene in Boulogne was a feeble one, easily rebuffed by the English. Halting on finding his approach to Calais barred by a detachment of Edward's force, Philip dithered for a few days and then retired. It was July. Next month, the citizens of Calais surrendered.

Their ability to resist for a year against an invader who, in a single afternoon, had annihilated the royal army of France, added point to the reluctance of contemporary commanders to expend time and resources tackling fortifications; conversely, it strengthened their reluctance to emerge from strongholds and give battle unless the odds favoured them heavily.

The frustrations of maintaining the siege were illustrated in its sequel, popularized by the story of Queen Philippa's compassion toward the citizens. So angered was Edward, it was said, by the prolonged defence that he determined to slay the entire population of Calais. On more temperate counsel, he limited sentence to the execution of the mayor and burgesses; finally, on the intercession of his wife, he granted complete amnesty.

Events determined a further truce. Edward's expedition was exhausted. Calais, which was to remain an English bastion in northern France for two centuries, was secured by a garrison and a nucleus of colonists. The belated re-embarkation of Edward's

Opposite The Black Prince: effigy in Canterbury Cathedral

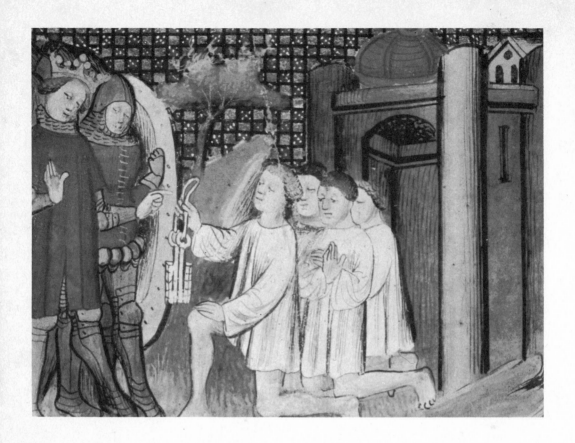

force was now imperative, as was his attention to home affairs.

Philip, for his own part, needed time to raise money and rebuild his fleet and army. Compounding the setbacks of Crécy and Calais, his ally David of Scotland had been defeated and captured by the English border lords at Neville's Cross, near Durham, in October 1346. His prestige tarnished, the French king lost much popularity.

At a meeting of the States-General, the representative assembly of France, three months after the capitulation of Calais, Philip was obliged to beg to gain even vague promises of finance. The States spokesman admonished him in plain terms: 'You went to these places [Crécy and Calais] in great company, at great cost and at great expense, and you were sent back scurvily, in shame, granting truces even while the enemy was in your kingdom ... you have been dishonoured.'

The time had come, the assembly considered, to punish Edward on his own soil. But when the king sent his commissioners through the country to raise money for the venture, the little they obtained had been spent before they came back. The invasion of England

62

was not a reality. Apart from lack of finance, France was paralysed by a new curse which, afflicting the English as cruelly, made warfare impracticable on both sides for several years.

At the end of 1347 the epidemic known as the Black Death appeared at Languedoc, in the far south of France, introduced, so the chroniclers had it, by a ship from the Middle East.

It seems to have been a mixture of bubonic and pneumonic plague. Small black pustules were noted on its victims, who died within a short time of first showing symptoms. No treatment was known for it.

Europe was ripe for diffusion of such a plague. In villages, and even more in urban areas, people lived in warren-like intimacy, negligent of hygiene, lacking proper sanitation. The disease spread alarmingly. During 1348 it swept the length of France and reached England, at first in the south-west. According to the contemporary and anonymous monk of Malmesbury, the pestilence entered at the port of Melcolme (Weymouth), which had supplied ships for the siege of Calais.

Another scribe, Robert of Avesbury, observed: 'It passed most rapidly from place to place, swiftly killing without respect of person, allowing the stricken no more than three, at most four days to live.'

Within months, the greatest harm the rival monarchs could have hoped to inflict on each other's kingdoms had been exceeded by the hand of a mocking fate. Some French towns lost half their inhabitants in the year. A typical Burgundian village was reduced from 1,200 to less than 600 people in four months. Land became fallow for want of labour. Women and children struggled behind ploughs.

In England, the port of Bristol came to a standstill, 'struck as it were by sudden death', declared the Leicester cleric Henry Knighton.

> Death broke forth on every side with the course of the sun. There died at Leicester in the small parish of St Leonard more than 380; in the parish of Holy Cross more than 400; in the parish of St Margaret more than 700; and so in each parish a great number. Then the bishop of Lincoln sent through the whole bishopric and gave general power to all and every priest, both regular and secular, to hear confessions ... Likewise, the pope granted full remission of all sins to whoever was absolved in peril of death, and everyone could choose a confessor at his will.

War was not a priority issue of the aftermath. Old enemies had become common sufferers. With the first wave of anguish and confusion, hostility found less rational outlets: alleged sorcerers and supposedly pollutant minorities. Jews were persecuted. Death and dislocation amid the law forces brought a sharp incline of crime in both countries, accompanied by a decline of moral leadership attendant on the decimation of the clergy.

In the longer term, economic disruption upset war policies. Big landlords, starved of labour and income by the death of their workmen and tenants, could not meet their martial obligations. Castles fell into decay. Knights, especially in France, took to brigandage for a livelihood. Diminished feeding stuffs were reserved for beasts more productive than battle steeds.

Inflation resulted. Scarcity of produce brought rising prices followed by demands for high wages which employers, unable to find adequate labour, could not resist. To arrest the spiral, both French and English monarchies introduced legislative measures of varying effectiveness. Anticipating the Statute of Labourers by two years, Westminster issued a first ordinance in 1349.

> The king sent proclamation into all the counties that reapers and other labourers should not take more than they had been accustomed to take, under a penalty appointed by statute. But the workmen were so uppity and obstinate that they would not listen to the king's command, but if any one wished to employ them he had to give them what they wanted, to satisfy their lofty and covetous wishes or lose his fruit and other crops. And when it was known to the king that some had not observed his command, and had given greater wages to the labourers, he levied heavy fines on abbots, priors, knights and other great folk and small folk ... (Henry Knighton).

Such measures, binding peasants and artisans – the great body of tax-payers – to penurious standards, reduced tax yields accordingly. The incapacity of the belligerent sovereigns to support military operations was acknowledged by almost a decade of truces following Calais, and campaigning, when resumed, was dogged by financial blight. Indeed, the disparity between ambition and resources

Opposite A Continental 'plague cross'

went far to explain the war's longevity.

The soil had barely settled on the victims of the Black Death when Philip of France died. At a time when shock and crisis set a premium on elevated leadership, the succession of John II in 1350 did the kingdom no service. True, he had titles, a dashing aspect, a name for martial gallantry. He prized the image of chivalry. The nobility of Europe sought his court for its tourneys and sumptuous feasts. He formed the *Chevaliers de l'Étoile*, an order famed for its

Overleaf The Black Death, a symbolic illustration

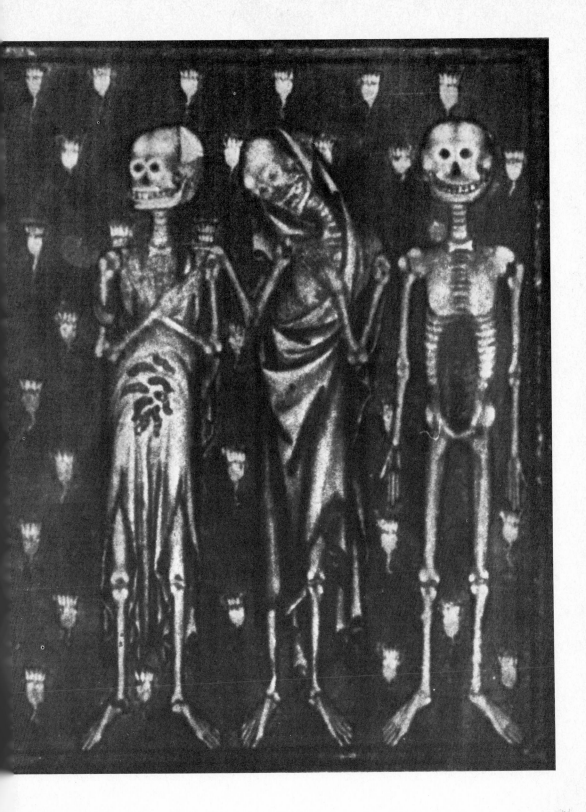

knightly airs and festivities. History called him John the Good.

It might have passed as a euphemism for mediocrity had he lacked a conspicuously vicious streak. His temper was paroxysmal, his antipathies irrational. The violent justice he dispensed was offset by no generous afterthought. Nor, despite his knightly posturing, had he shown much military competence as Duke of Normandy.

Worse for the kingdom, John was terrified by the problems he inherited, the realities crowding the mirage of his brilliant court. And apprehension was justified – but the near-panic of the king did not help.

Agricultural workers, threatened with branding unless they toiled for low rates, fled the manors of their lords, who then accused the government of ruining them. Savage sentences against suspect vassals, engendered by an atmosphere of regal paranoia, prevented neither Charles of Blois, John's cousin, nor Charles of Navarre, his son-in-law, conspiring with Edward. The introduction of unannounced inspections of French army companies to ensure they behaved themselves was useless when the king could not pay the troops.

With the royal forces in disarray, the royal currency devalued seventy per cent since the Black Death, and Edward shrewdly feeding his rival's fears with demands and threats, John was soon at his wits' end. Almost no price, it seems, was too high for a respite – excluding the resumption of warfare.

In April 1354, at Guines, John's diplomats agreed terms for a conclusive peace. They were staggering, for while Edward merely renounced his empty pretensions to the French crown John granted Edward not only Guienne but Poitou, Touraine, Anjou, Maine and Normandy, all in full sovereignty. At a stroke, the King of France had surrendered half his kingdom.

Whether such a settlement could have been enforced is problematic, since it was never ratified. Stiffened by English violations in Brittany, John had pulled himself together sufficiently by the autumn to withdraw the bargain. Humiliated, his word broken, the French sovereign awaited war: the war he dreaded, and for which he was unprepared.

Edward was confident. Unlike France, England had emerged from the disaster of the plague with continuity of leadership and a diminution, thanks to the capture of the Scottish king, of its peripheral problems. Measures against economic disruption, though imperfect, were more effective in England than on the Continent. If resources were slender, the spirit of military enter-

prise stirred anew in king and magnates. In 1355, Edward took the offensive, delegating the effort in Guienne to the Black Prince.

 The youth of Crécy was now twenty-five, in theory a fine soldier. He had competed in jousts, designed equipment for his war steeds, disported armour swathed in rich velvet, and lavished gifts on his

The coronation of John II of France

69

lieutenants. The youngest member, in his time, of the Order of the Garter, he was versed minutely in the doctrines of chivalry.

That he was also a reckless gambler and spendthrift, heavily in debt by his twenties, with a chilling indifference to much human suffering, was not held against him by the chroniclers. By their lights, the prince was the epitome of knightliness. Still, he had come to manhood during the truce. He had yet to prove his generalship in action.

The expedition to Guienne was not large, but could expect the support of Gascon forces. Rather less than 3,000 men are thought to have disembarked at Bordeaux, including something like 1,000 lances, 1,700 archers and 170 Welsh infantry. Significant in the composition was the high proportion of archers, reflecting the rising value placed on missile tactics, and the extent to which the army was mounted: 1,000 of the archers were provided with horses for the line of march.

Of four leading magnates who accompanied the Black Prince – the Earls of Oxford, Suffolk, Warwick and Salisbury – the first three were middle-aged veterans with a weighty aggregate of war experience, and all had served at Crécy and Calais. For the rest, the force comprised nobles and commoners from Westmorland and Yorkshire to the southern shires, with a notable inclusion of criminals: murderers, rapists, abductors and thieves were mentioned.

At Bordeaux, a port firmly loyal to the English king, they were joined by Gascon troops, and contingents from neighbouring Bearn, under the barons of south-west France. Especially prominent was the Captal (Lord) of Buch, Jean de Grailly, a leader with an outstanding military record. Familiar with the country and the enemy, the Gascons were invaluable as advisers to the English prince.

The plan concocted at Bordeaux was simple. The French king's lieutenant in the region of Languedoc, Jean Count of Armagnac, had embittered the Gascon lords by actions at their expense. It was resolved, 'by advice and counsel of all the lords with us', as the prince wrote, to take revenge by ravaging Armagnac, the buffer county between Guienne and Languedoc.

Though monotonous in its depredations, the ensuing enterprise proceeded with a breathless quality reminiscent less of Edward's leisurely advance of 1346 than of the swift and savage *routier* rampage the French called a *chevaucher de guerre*, a 'war ride'. The onset of autumn – the force did not set off until late September – created urgency. In the first week of October, advancing to the frontier, the prince moved so rapidly that 'many horses were lost' – driven too hard after an unhealthy journey in ships' holds. In the second week, they passed Arouille, the last town before the border, unfurled their banners and burst upon Armagnac.

The countryside, sloping gently from the southerly Pyrenees to the plain of the Garonne, was, as Baker of Swinbrook put it, 'rich and beautiful'. The *vendage*, the time of the grape harvest, was just over, the people contemplating the fruits of their hard work. It went for nothing as the invaders struck, burning, looting, murdering. In rapid succession, they hit the frontier towns of Monclar and Estang, then thrust deeper to Plaisance, plundering the local produce, destroying the growing vines.

Careering east across the great skein of tributaries feeding the Garonne, the Black Prince left a trail of devastation through Armagnac. No army moved to meet him. The count had been at Agen, near the border, with a force of royal troops, as the prince approached, but had withdrawn up the Garonne toward Toulouse and Languedoc – perhaps doubtful of his strength, or fearful of the enemy's mobility.

Within twelve days of entering the county, the Anglo–Gascon force had traversed its breadth, 'harrying and wasting the land', as the prince wrote, 'whereby the [Gascon] lieges of our most honoured king were much gratified'. But not, it seems, sated. For having ravaged the count's possessions the invaders maintained their momentum towards Toulouse and the count himself.

There was a certain intoxication in their resolve. Within the walls of the regional capital a sorely insulted Count of Armagnac had prepared thoroughly. Royal and local troops stood at readiness. Bridges had been broken. Outlying buildings had been erased to deny the raiders shelter. Militarily, the risks of proceeding were great, but the lure was great also.

Beyond Toulouse and the protective arc of the broad Garonne lay the bountiful vales of Languedoc, stretching tranquilly to Narbonne and the Mediterranean. Once across the river, the despoilers would be among people, in Baker's words, of 'unwarlike temperament', softened by security. The way would be easy, the pickings lush.

Overleaf The Black Death: Burial of the dead at Tournai, 1349

The English and Gascons took a gamble. On 28 October, in a single concerted rush, they left St Lys, south-west of Toulouse, marched ten miles to the Garonne, rode straight into the stream and struggled to the far bank, marched two miles to a second river, the Ariège, plunged through that and stopped at last at a place named La Croix Falgarde.

Miles to the north-west, the bypassed forces of Toulouse were incredulous. 'Never before,' exclaimed Baker, 'had horsed troops crossed those waters.' According to the chronicler, the Garonne was terrifying; the Ariège, narrower but swifter, still more dangerous. Both had claimed victims. Nor was the peril entirely passed, for sooner or later the obstacles would have to be recrossed. Meanwhile, Languedoc lay at the mercy of the Black Prince.

The raiders raced east toward Narbonne. The catalogue of rape and ruin is repetitive. Montiscard, Avignonet and Mas Saintes Puelles were burned, the last with its abbey. A church,

74

hospital and two convents were destroyed at Castlenaudary. Barns and cottages were gutted, windmills smashed. Most of the people fled. Some, thought worthy of ransom, were rounded up and, failing payment, butchered.

Carcassonne, an important town on the River Aude, was crowded with refugees hopeful that its castle would offer security. It did not. Ignoring both the castle and an essay to buy off the invaders, the Black Prince sacked and destroyed the conurbation. Trebes, to the east, shared its fate, devastated along with its surrounding farms.

Finally, descending toward the Golfe du Lion, the plunder-laden column approached the ancient and flourishing trade centre of Narbonne. It was the first week of November. In just over a month, the expedition had covered about 300 miles across southern France, from coast to coast, virtually unchallenged, demonstrably unchecked.

Narbonne produced the first disconcerting resistance to the prince's troops. A barrage of heavy missiles from the citadel greeted the occupation of the civil quarters, where enjoyment of large supplies of food and wine was interrupted by regular ballista fire. When assaults on the stronghold proved futile, the invaders fired the adjacent dwellings and withdrew to the countryside. It was now time for a review of the prince's objectives.

The Constable of France was manoeuvring to intercept the Anglo-Gascon force. French troops were reported advancing from Montpellier. The Count of Armagnac's lieutenants were no more than a few miles in the prince's rear. His wagons were being harried by bands of daring Narbonnais. There could be no doubt that an immediate turn-about was indicated. From now on, the primary aim of the expedition was extrication, the return of men and booty to friendly soil.

That is not to say that demolition and plunder were neglected. Many places were hit on the march west. But there was less urge to linger in the process. By mid-November, wearying day-long rides and poor camps marked the emphasis on making ground. The weather was deteriorating. Rivers had to be crossed before the winter floods.

From Narbonne, the raiders had looped north. Now they veered south-west, cutting their outward path near Carcassonne on the way to describing a horizontal figure of eight across Languedoc. 75

English pike-head

Beyond the intersection, they marched some way beside the lands
of the Count of Foix, a noble of studied neutrality with no love for
his neighbour Jean of Armagnac.

Passing the Foix estates on their best behaviour, the marauders
gave Toulouse a wide berth, crossing the Ariège at Miremont,
prudently fording the Garonne well upstream. The passage was
timely. Heavy rain had begun to fall, and the river was impassable
next day. Thankfully, the troops fell out on the west bank to
recuperate. It was their first real respite since leaving Narbonne.

The rest of November was a scramble. Rain continued to fall as the hours of daylight shortened. From Toulouse and further north, hostile forces converged by the narrow and sodden lanes. On Thursday 19 November, the Constable of France and the Count of Armagnac camped within two leagues (perhaps five miles) of the raiders. On Friday, an Anglo–Gascon patrol of eighty lances skirmished with one of several French columns dogging the prince's force. English soldiers could see the enemy's camp fires that evening.

Bearing north again to cross their outward path near Aurade, the invaders threw themselves determinedly at the battery of flooded tributaries lacing Armagnac. Fords and bridges had to be sought, strongholds skirted. They were ready now, at any time, to be called to battle stations. For several hours on the 23rd, they adopted fighting formation, expecting a strong attack.

In fact, it did not materialize. The rivers were hindering the pursuit as much as the withdrawal. There was friction, too, in the French camp. The Constable and Count Jean were at loggerheads over the latter's failure to halt the raiders earlier. When the expedition passed its last major barrier, the swollen Gers, on the 25th, the likelihood of being overhauled had faded. On 28 November, having rested at Réjaumont, the Black Prince emerged from the woods of western Armagnac to the friendly outpost of Mezin. Ahead, the moors of Guienne betokened the raid's successful outcome.

Military historians of a later age, demanding battles, have underestimated the campaign. But it was the very avoidance of serious confrontation during so deep a penetration of hostile territory that made the exploit a classic of medieval raiding. For all the repugnance now evoked by its squalid destructiveness, the triumph of the offensive was unqualified. The King of France and his southern lords had been acutely humiliated. The desolation of many towns, including the rich centres of Carcassonne and Narbonne, together with hundreds of miles of prime farmland, was a serious blow to John's revenues, for the region had been a valuable source of taxation.

Then the raid had enriched its participants. In plunder and ransom money, the gains were considerable. 'The prince and his men had great profit,' observed Froissart. Much of it went to the Gascons, whom the chronicler regarded as a grasping lot. But doubtless the prince was satisfied. Edward's French liegemen, having tasted the rewards of loyalty, were eager for a further venture. They would yet have a battle to talk about. 77

Chapter 5

The Campaign of Poitiers

The French failure to move decisively against the Anglo–Gascon campaign of 1355 could be explained, at least in part, by fear of greater danger in the north of France. That summer, Edward's cousin and lieutenant, Henry Duke of Lancaster, had sailed from the Thames estuary with an army bound for Normandy. Encountering difficulties, the fleet eventually put into Southampton, but its intentions had caused John anxiety. And in November, as the Black Prince headed for Narbonne, Edward had landed at Calais with another force.

Threatened north and south, the French king had thrown his main resources towards the senior and most immediate of his adversaries, marching to meet the King of England. As it happened, Edward withdrew unexpectedly. The Scots had taken Berwick, and his forces were needed there. But he had diverted French attention from his son's raid.

It must be said that John acted sensibly. While the Anglo–Gascon success was, of its nature, limited and remote from central government, the English northern projects were potentially critical. Their abortion gave cause for satisfaction at the French court.

Less comforting to John was the behaviour of an unpleasant son-in-law, Charles of Navarre, a descendant of the last direct Capetians. Young, glib and covetous, Charles had been born too late to prevent the Valois succession, and could not forget it. His small kingdom of Navarre, plus a few Norman fiefs, did not console him. Nor had his marriage, in 1352, to John's daughter. Too weak to challenge his father-in-law directly, Charles engaged in a policy of intrigue with England, using the threat of an alliance with Edward to extort concessions from his relative. John, afraid of opening old divisions in the kingdom, concealed his fury, but forbearance proved a thankless course.

By 1354 Charles was seeking armed aid from the Duke of Lancaster. John bought momentary reconciliation (the Treaty of Mantes) with a slice of Cotentin. Next year, when Charles again turned to England, John appeased him with the Treaty of Valognes.

The younger man promptly repaid the sovereign by establishing a subversive friendship with John's heir, the dauphin Charles, newly created Duke of Normandy. Tale had it that the two bloods, revelling at Rouen, were actually plotting the king's demise. John could control himself no longer. Riding secretly to Rouen in April 1356, he surprised his son and son-in-law banqueting. A

Opposite Sir John Chandos

80   Battle of Poitiers: symbolic illumination

number of those present were executed on the spot. Charles of Navarre was dragged to prison.

The stroke, long invited, provoked a storm in Normandy, where John's weakness toward his son-in-law had encouraged intrigue among the captious nobility. Charles's brother, Philip of Navarre, appealing to England for help against the French king, was quickly gratified. In June Lancaster succeeded in landing a raiding force at la Hogue. Abetted by the anti-Valois faction of the duchy, it was soon marching deep into Normandy.

Lancaster reached Verneuil, about sixty-five miles west of Paris, before John's approach put a stop to the advance. It was not the duke's intention to engage a royal army. Instead, he reversed with alacrity to Cotentin, leaving John to mop up dissident Norman elements in his path. Thus, in consecutive years, both Lancaster and Edward himself had withdrawn before the King of France.

If their motivation was less awe-inspired than French loyalists might have liked to think, it was a much needed fillip to John's morale. In August he turned at last to the south and the Black Prince.

The winter following the Anglo–Gascon raid of 1355 was one of small-scale operations in the southern marchlands. Jean of Armagnac, undefeated if mortified, looked anew at his western defences. The Prince of Wales sought to exploit his psychological advantage by coercion and bribery aimed at the border lords. Some switched sides in his favour. Others, sticking to their colours, were harassed.

Contemporary reports of these operations, though less detailed than those of the big summer campaigns, give some idea of the unseasonal military activities of this period. Divided into light groups under individual captains, the prince's troops struck over a wide area at Cognac, Perigueux, Agen, Mirabeau, and elsewhere. The north bank of the Garonne, undisturbed in the autumn raid, became the hunting ground for detachments operating 100 miles and more from Bordeaux. Seventeen castles and several towns were taken in this region.

Particularly noted were the achievements of Sir John Chandos and Sir James Audley, the prince's 'chief advisers'. Chandos, a crown officer with Cheshire connections, was arguably the outstanding soldier in the prince's suite. His long military career, which concluded only with his death in 1370, is emblazoned with personal victories. Audley, who held land in Devon among other shires, was highly rated as a captain by Edward III.

During the winter, they worked together in the capture of holds in the Garonne valley, joining the formidable Captal of Buch to besiege Perigueux. The respect accorded the experienced Gascon is witnessed by the fact that it was he who commanded the English troops who eventually took the town.

At headquarters, it was a time of planning forward to fair weather, reviewing manpower requirements and logistics. The Black Prince sent home his needs for the coming spring: men, missile arms and certain food supplies.

In reinforcements, he was competing for satisfaction with Edward and Lancaster. It was arranged to send him a further 500 Cheshire archers and 100 from Gloucester. These had to be recruited, clothed, armed and conveyed to Plymouth during the winter. Fletchers were commissioned to produce 1,000 bows, 2,000 sheaves of arrows and 400 gross of bowstrings to refurbish the prince's force. Fresh horses were also ordered, and grooms sought to sail with them. Quantities of food were assembled for shipment. Among other victuals, corn and salted pork were loaded on the transports awaiting a fair wind for southern France. Like most medieval war requisitions, they arrived late.

The sea convoy reached Bordeaux not by spring but in mid-June, almost simultaneously with the start of Lancaster's northern raid. It was August before the Anglo–Gascon army was ready to embark on its second major venture, the 'war ride' that was to culminate on the field of Poitiers.

It has been suggested that in heading north towards the rich Loire valley of central France, the prince aimed at a conjunction with Lancaster. Neither the methods nor the communications of the age supported the idea of such a plan. Indeed, so far as the two expeditions were able to keep in touch across hostile territory, it would have been known to Prince Edward at an early stage that Lancaster was already retiring. If John pursued him, the southern force would have a free rein. Should the French king turn south to repulse the Anglo–Gascon raid, then Normandy would again become vulnerable to Lancaster, or to a landing by the English king.

In short, to the extent that a strategy existed, it was one of playing audacious mice to the French cat, of inflicting damage to north and south at the same time and depending on mobility to escape disaster when the cat pounced. 'It was our purpose to ride

forth,' wrote the prince, 'against our enemies in the parts of
France.' Riding against enemies meant the customary process of
opportunistic destruction and plunder. Specific objectives were
not implied.

When a substantial guard had been detached to protect Guienne
in the prince's absence, the marauding army numbered perhaps
7,000 fighting men, or rather less. This total is generally estimated
in the proportion of about 3,500 men-at-arms, 2,500 archers and
1,000 lightly armed foot troops. At least half, and probably more,
were Gascons, these preponderant among the knights while the
English contributed most of the archers. As before, the majority of
bowmen – therefore, the bulk of the force itself – were mounted.

On 4 August 1356, the army began an advance which, to its
northern extremity, was to cover more than 200 miles of road
across Limousin, Marche and Berri to the heart of John's kingdom.
By the middle of the month, it had passed the watershed of the
Dordogne and Loire valleys by way of Brantôme, Rochechouart,
Lesterp and Bellac, and was making for Lussac les Eglises and
Argenton. Throughout August, the incursion progressed unimpeded. On the 28th, having crossed the River Indre by Chateauroux, the prince reached the River Cher at Vierzon, concluding
the northern leg.

Ahead lay the wild, sparsely populated land of the Sologne between the Cher and Loire valleys. Upstream to the east was Bourges, a strongly fortified city held, it was believed, by John's son, the Count of Poitiers. It was decided to turn west down the Cher, following the stream to Tours and the Loire itself.

By way of digression, a strong cavalry detachment under Audley and Chandos sallied north and sacked and burned Aubigny. As the party was returning to the main force, it met a band of French mercenaries commanded by one Philip de Chambly, known as Gris Mouton, or Grey Mutton. From prisoners taken in the ensuing skirmish, the English learned for the first time that John was mustering an army at Chartres.

This news did not dismay the prince's camp. Between Chartres and the Cher lay the wilds of the Sologne and the broad Loire. Bridges were far apart. Even in a straight line, there were about eighty miles between the armies, and John would have to detour to find a suitable crossing place. Moreover, the French forces would need some days to organize before starting south. All considered, the raiders were taking no great risk in continuing west to Tours, about seventy miles from Vierzon, before turning on to a homeward course. More questionable was their sluggish pace.

Having spent four days besieging a castle at Romorantin, slightly north of the Cher, and a further four days beneath the walls of Tours, it was 11 September before the prince started south for Bordeaux. Confident of out-marching a cumbersome French royal army, the marauders had frittered their lead away. Thirty miles to the north-east, John had already crossed the Loire at Blois.

In fact, the French force had not descended to the Loire in a single mass but had divided into a number of more manoeuvrable units, approaching the river on a wide front. While the king crossed at Blois, other corps had made use of bridges at Orleans, Meung, Tours and near Saumer. From these, it had converged in pursuit, of the enemy to the south.

The leading body of the French army – the powerful division with the king himself – advanced at a testing pace. On 13 and 14 September, John covered a total of forty miles to arrive at La Haye, thirty miles from Tours, within hours of the prince's departure. Despite its greater potential for mobility, the Anglo–Gascon force was travelling at a slower speed.

On the 14th, the Black Prince made little more than ten miles to Chatellerault, on the Poitiers–Bordeaux road. Extraordinarily, as it now seems, he stayed there for two days.

It should be remembered, however, that the expectation of dynamic intervention had hardly been a feature of Anglo–Gascon operations in southern France. Neither Jean of Armagnac nor the Constable of France had been effective in pursuit during the preceding raid. Experience made for complacency. It was not so much John as Poitiers, a formidable stronghold in the raiders' path, which preoccupied the prince's scouts.

That his information was poor emerges from the annals. Starting south again on the 17th, the Black Prince 'wist not truly where the French were'. John was little better posted by his own scouts. The preliminaries to Poitiers evoke a curious likeness to blind-man's-buff.

Immediately south of Chatellerault, the confluence of the Rivers Clain and Vienne may be pictured as the apex of a rough triangle based on Poitiers and Chauvigny. The Clain, running through Poitiers, forms the west side; the Vienne, through Chauvigny, the east side. Within this triangle, the raiders descended from Chatellerault. Outside it, to the east, John made directly for Chauvigny from La Haye. A few miles apart, the two armies were marching on parallels, neither certain of the other's whereabouts.

John, at least, made a good guess. Correctly, he assumed that if he hastened to the bridge at Chauvigny, then turned west and closed the gap between there and Poitiers, the Black Prince must be trapped somewhere in the fork formed by the two streams. Reaching Chauvigny on the 17th, as the prince departed Chatellerault, the French were ideally placed to spring the trap.

At this point, poor intelligence again confused the issue. Having crossed the Vienne, John became convinced that his quarry had already escaped south. In consequence, he continued without delay to Poitiers, which he entered early on Saturday the 18th. His rear were still streaming west on the Chauvigny–Poitiers road when the Anglo–Gascon vanguard approached their right flank. Extricating themselves from a brief mêlée, the antagonists galloped to alert their respective leaders.

The Black Prince, having narrowly escaped disaster, remained in peril. Every mile he could put between himself and Poitiers was now vital, but he had marched hard that day and the hour was late. Apprehensively, he crossed the king's road, pushed on a mile or two through wooded, undulating countryside, then camped by the village of Savigny l'Evescault.

That evening, the Captal of Buch rode north-west to reconnoitre Poitiers. The scene he discovered left no doubt of the imminence of danger. The French army was arrayed south-east of the city, 85

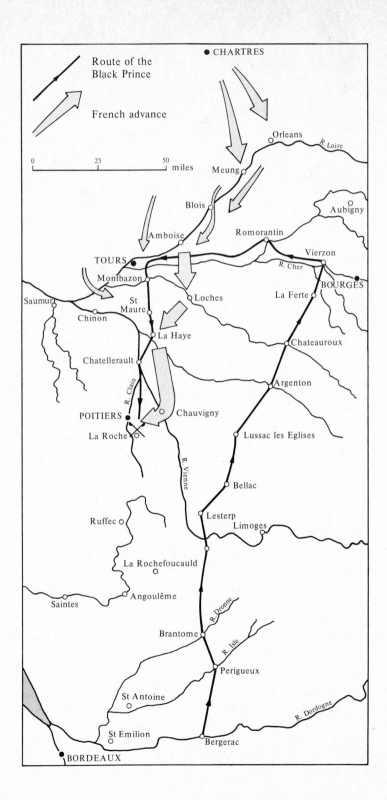

Route of the
Black Prince

French advance

● CHARTRES

Orleans

R. Loire

Meung

Blois

Amboise

Aubigny

Romorantin

Vierzon

R. Cher

BOURGES

TOURS

Montbazon

Saumur

Chinon

St
Maure

Loches

La Ferte

La Haye

Chateauroux

Chatellerault

R. Clain

Argenton

POITIERS

Chauvigny

La Roche

Lussac les Eglises

R. Vienne

Bellac

Ruffec

Lesterp

Limoges

La Rochefoucauld

Angoulême

R. Dronne

Saintes

Brantome

R. Isle

Perigueux

St Antoine

R. Dordogne

St Emilion

Bergerac

BORDEAUX

ready to resume pursuit at first light. The Gascon reported an awesome force: 'All the plain was covered with men-at-arms.'

As usual, numerical estimates of the French host differ, though contemporary sources are unanimous in making it vastly the greater of the armies at Poitiers. Modern analysts put it at about 16,000 men, well over double the Anglo–Gascon strength. With possibly 8,000 men-at-arms, the French king's force outnumbered all ranks of the enemy in these alone. In light infantry, it dominated by something like six to one. Only in missile troops – 2,000 cross-bowmen to 2,500 archers – was it the smaller body.

On top of such discrepancies, the prince had supply problems. An arduous march from Chatellerault, interrupted by skirmishing, had left little time for foraging. Savigny was too small a place to offer much food, nor had it a stream at which to water the horses. Men and animals passed the night hungrily and thirstily.

Dawn on Sunday 19 September presented the raiders with a hard choice: either to embark, jaded and unrefreshed, on a race to keep ahead of John's army, or to fight an early defensive action and pray for the fortune of Crécy.

The prince's counsellors compromised. Saddling early, the force moved a short distance south to a place named Nouaillé, mainly notable for its Benedictine abbey, where a fair defensive site was enhanced by fresh food supplies and a stream, the Miosson, for the horses. If the French came up quickly, at least they might be delayed here. Failing an immediate approach, the raiders were conveniently placed to slip away towards Bordeaux, screened by a background of woods and the Miosson, a steep-banked branch of the River Clain. Escape was the priority. The second great land battle of the Hundred Years War, like its predecessor of 1346, was to be no choice of a Plantagenet.

From Nouaillé, the road to Poitiers ran north-west through a screening wood, emerged on open land near a spot known as Maupertuis ('bad road'), crossed a shallow declivity draining to the Miosson on the left, and continued perhaps a mile and a half to where, on Sunday, the French encamped. Straddling the road at the head of the slight slope at Maupertuis, the English front was defined by a hedge of some thousand yards bordering vines and other crops.

Broadly, the surrounding land was flat, a plateau rather more than 400 feet above sea level, but on the left of the defensive front it

Fighting at Poitiers

dropped fairly sharply through fifty feet or more to the Miosson. On the right, somewhat behind the front position, a grassy hummock rose gently to 440 feet.

The Anglo–Gascon force was disposed in the customary three 'battles', the foremost lining the hedge under the command of Buch, Warwick and Oxford, the reserve towards the wood in the charge of Salisbury and Suffolk, and the centre headed by the Black Prince with Audley, Chandos and those Gascon leaders who were not in the front line. As at Crécy, the archers were deployed to the fore in saw-edged, or 'harrow', formation, some in trenches. All participants in the defence were to fight on foot. While the Miosson covered the left flank, the right was more open, and here a portion of the wagon fleet was stationed to impede the enemy.

The day was still young when approaching riders were spotted. These, it transpired, were not French troops but members of a papal embassy led by the cardinal Hélie de Talleyrand-Perigord, who had followed the campaign from the Loire south. Bent on arranging terms between the two camps, Talleyrand achieved a truce for the Sunday. The prince was not loath to treat. Indeed, according to report he was ready to abandon all the gains of the raid to extricate himself, offering not only the return of booty and prisoners but a pledge to refrain from fighting the French king for seven years.

John had less incentive to negotiate. It had cost him much in treasure and toil to confront his quarry. With the odds over-whelmingly in his favour, nothing less than the personal surrender of the Black Prince, together with a hundred leading knights of the raiding force, would satisfy him. On such conditions, the cardinal's last-minute bid for peace floundered.

On Sunday night, the prince's war council pondered the morrow. Against a persisting desire for retreat, if feasible, was an increased reluctance, in view of defensive preparations advanced in the truce period, to abandon Maupertuis lightly. The plan agreed appears to have embraced cautious steps towards with-drawal, at the same time envisaging a bold defence, or rearguard action, if needs be.

As a first step, the most valuable of the baggage, loaded on such wagons as could be spared from the right flank, was to be moved to the south of the Miosson escorted by the Earl of Warwick's troops. Here, sheltered by woods, the heavy vehicles would be close to the Bordeaux road. The manoeuvre was probably planned with the bridge in Nouaillé village as a crossing point, though a supple-mentary passage (Gue de l'Homme, or Man's Ford) was available upstream, nearer the English front.

During this process, every soldier not involved was to stand at readiness in case of a French attack. It has been argued that the removal of the wagons under escort was a ruse to provoke a premature assault by the enemy. While the theory is not incom-patible with a getaway strategy, it seems on the evidence a doubtful rationalization of what transpired.

Early on Monday, a day unremarked for exceptional weather, the French army moved forward. The chronicles conjure up a 89

splendid scene. John's flag, the oriflamme, was carried by the Lord of Charny, whose own red banner and silver escutcheons were borne beside him. On all sides, the knights of France, vying in magnificence, could be identified by their armorial bearings: 'gold, azure, purple, gules and ermine.' Burnished helmets and shields gleamed. 'There might have been seen,' observed Froissart, 'great nobleness of fair harness and rich armoury, banners and pennons.'

The host advanced in three main bodies. In the rear, with the largest formation, was the king himself. Ahead, commanding impressive divisions, were the dauphin Charles, Duke of Normandy, and the king's brother, the Duke of Orleans. In the van rode a special shock force including 300 of the hardiest and most experienced French knights led by two of John's best commanders, the marshals Arnoul d'Audrehem and Jean de Clermont. The novel composition of this vanguard had been decided by a report on the enemy position.

Sunday had provided ample opportunity for reconnaissance. Observation of the hedge at the English front, open only for the narrow width of its bisecting road, and lined with archers and dismounted knights, had persuaded John to abandon traditional tactics. Instead of a massed cavalry onslaught, the attack would be opened by a small and select unit of horsemen, supported by bowmen, commissioned to force a breach in the defensive line. Behind would come the customary waves of chivalry – on foot.

John's unexpected decision to employ his knights largely as infantry appears to have stemmed from several influences. Memories of Crécy, a dramatic victory for dismounted troops, were still vivid. Accounts of infantry ascendancy at Halidon and other Scottish battles were known to the King of France. Indeed, a prominent Scot, the Earl of Douglas, was with John at Poitiers.

Substantial precedent could be produced to support the value of dismounted action, but one aspect of the evidence seems to have eluded John: English knights had succeeded on foot in defensive, not offensive, engagement. Where infantry had attacked effectively in the Scottish wars, it had comprised pikemen rather than men-at-arms. The feasibility of using heavily armoured knights in foot assault was dubious. Events were to make this point.

The day started conventionally. Soon after sunrise, an Anglo–Gascon patrol led by one Eustace Daubriggecourt made contact with the French van. In the mounted skirmish which ensued, Daubriggecourt was captured. The 300 picked knights leading John's army rode forward, topped a modest rise between the two camps and looked across the depression to their front at the prince's position.

The enemy, as it appeared to them, was in two parts: one gathered before the wood of Nouaillé, the other (Warwick's escort and the loaded wagons) preparing to cross the Miosson. It may well be that the French thought they had surprised a withdrawing force for which the line concealed by the hedge was a thinly spread rearguard. At all events, the reaction was divided. Of the two marshals commanding the French horse, Audrehem favoured action, Clermont advised caution.

The former had his way. Inclining to the right, Audrehem led his section of the vanguard towards the retiring wagons while Clermont headed for the stationary body of the enemy. The charge was disastrous.

As Audrehem's knights streamed headlong for the Miosson, the unprotected flanks of their mounts were exposed to the English archers. 'The horses, being galled and wounded, fell to tumbling 91

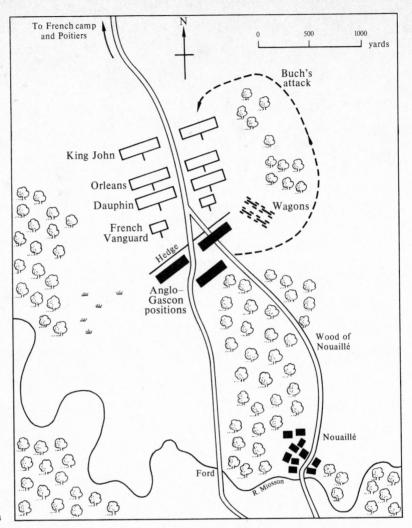

To French camp
and Poitiers

N

0   500   1000
yards

Buch's
attack

King John

Orleans

Dauphin

French
Vanguard

Wagons

Hedge

Anglo–
Gascon
positions

Wood of
Nouaillé

Nouaillé

Ford

R. Miosson

Battle of Poitiers

with them that sat on their backs, or else turned and ran on them
that followed after.' Many riders were killed or, like Audrehem,
captured.

Clermont, galloping straight at the English line, was enfiladed
from either side by obliquely posted longbows. The deadliness of
the archers is stressed in the chronicles. 'They shot so thick that the
Frenchmen wist not on what side to take heed.' Along with
numerous companions, among them Gautier de Brienne, Constable
of France, Clermont perished in the charge.

The French van was demolished in its reckless rush. The battle
was barely open, yet three outstanding leaders and scores of the
kingdom's best fighters were lost to John. Equally bad, the assault

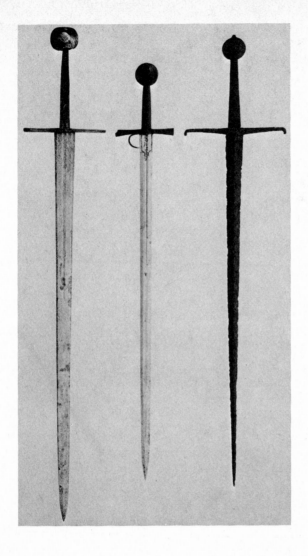

Three European swords
of the war period

and subsequent flight of the survivors masked the fire of the cross-
bowmen advancing in support of the cavalry. John's missile troops
were repulsed in confusion by their faster-shooting English
counterparts. The deficiency in French firepower thus became
radical.

Still, John's big battalions had yet to take the battlefield. As
Warwick's men hastened from the wagons to reinforce the prince's
front, the dauphin's division prepared to meet the enemy. Dismounted as ordained, its knights lumbered across the dipping
ground toward the line of hedge. They weathered the barrage of
English shafts with less damage than that sustained in the mounted
charge, but the weight of metal they carried was punishing.

Massacre of rebellious
French peasants at
Meaux, 1358, by the
Dauphin's troops

In a ponderous, creaking wave they broke on the waiting defence, muscles already aching beneath armour laboriously humped for several hundred yards. For the first time in the war, massed chivalry was locked in pedestrian battle. Froissart portrayed the clash as one of numerous local rallies and skirmishes, an epic struggle into which the Black Prince threw every man of his force save a reserve of 400. The noise was immense. Contemporary accounts tell how the French repeatedly roared 'Mountjoy! St Denis!' and the English responded with 'St George! Guienne!' 'They sounded their trumpets, one giving answer to another, making such a din that the walls of Poitiers sounded with the echo.'

Tabors and horns, the clash of steel and the cries of the wounded mingled in a tumult that was 'wonderful and terrible'. Many knights, thrown on their backs, lay as helpless as overturned beetles until their comrades could lift them up. Archers who had expended their arrows scavenged the field drawing shafts 'from poor wretches that were but half dead'. Others, discarding their bows, drew the knives from their belts and fell upon crippled or exhausted French men-at-arms.

The dauphin's troops fought valiantly, but they were less than a third of John's army and outnumbered by their adversaries. The French knights reached the affray already weary. Not much is told of the accompanying militia, but, untrained and ill armed, they can have had little heart for the hail of arrows which greeted them. Gradually, what remained of the French division withdrew.

Had John's second 'battle' advanced, albeit awkwardly, with the resolution of the first, the Anglo–Gascon defence must have despaired. Its casualties were heavy, its archers short of missiles. With no more than a few hundred fresh men, the Black Prince was poorly placed to face the Duke of Orleans and his powerful corps.

Incredibly, the moment passed in anti climax. To the surprise of contemporaries and the puzzlement of historians ever since, the duke and his knights mounted their horses and left the field. Writers of the time, though scornful, could not explain this odd move.

Plainly, it was not the result of any stampede. The dauphin's force, though mauled, had not been routed. Its survivors had drawn back with honour. The departure of Orleans's division was orderly. That the French army was eager for battle is evident. The king's vassals had joined him in large numbers. They had pressed the pursuit of the raiders with much energy. The ill fated vanguard had demonstrated its enthusiasm to a fault. Why, then, should almost a third of the host abscond without fighting?

The most plausible explanation reposes in the known resistance of martial groups to new modes of combat – here, the dismounting of cavalry in attack, an innovation for which the French were singularly unprepared. No chivalry in Europe placed greater emphasis on the ideals of knightly confrontation, the glories of equestrian warfare, than that of France. French noblemen trained, equipped and mounted themselves with consummate pride for cavalry engagement. If the practical problems of advancing on foot were anticipated by John's knights, these were perhaps less offensive to the spirit of French chivalry than the idea of being reduced to the level of common soldiers, of riff-raff. Without their caparisoned war steeds, there was no splendour, no chivalric honour in store for them.

Had John been present to set an example, his brother's division might have swallowed its pride and gone forward. Personal exhortation rather than indirect command was the better part of discipline in medieval battle. But the king was elsewhere, with the rear division. Denied the time-honoured dash to glory, Orleans and his nobles abandoned their sovereign.

Seen in perspective, the desertion turned the contest against John. At the time, it cannot have seemed critical. The Anglo–Gascon army had fought desperately for perhaps two hours and was ravaged by casualties. John's numerical advantage had withered, but his largest and best-ordered 'battle' was still fresh, advancing with the king as an enspiriting figurehead. Its approach, banners aloft, trumpets blaring, brought prayers from the defenders.

The breathing space granted by Orleans had been invaluable. Nevertheless, doubts that the French could be resisted were palpable. Legend enshrines them in the anecdote, perhaps apocryphal, that the Black Prince, overhearing a pessimistic comment, retorted that talk of defeat was blasphemy while he still lived.

Rather than further reduce morale by waiting for the French blow, drastic measures were counselled in the prince's camp. The wounded had been 'dragged under hedges and bushes out of the way'. The entire force still capable of fighting was now mounted, using wagon and sumpter horses where necessary, and prepared to sally at the enemy. Concomitant to this stroke, a small band of riders was to circle John's division by concealed ground and appear in the king's rear. The resourceful Buch took command of this special task.

With 'a right great shout', the erstwhile defenders spurred forward. Beside the prince rode his standard-bearer Woodland.

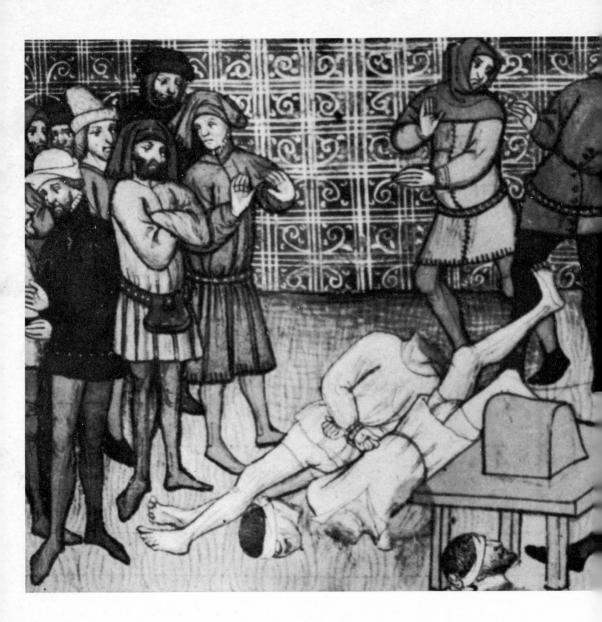

Ahead, robot-like in their mailed shells, the dismounted knights of France halted around the oriflamme of their sovereign. The roles had been interchanged. Fatigued by its advance, and lacking proper missile cover, John's chivalry stood on open land to receive the charge.

The second and climactic hand-to-hand struggle of the battle was thus engaged. It was, by all accounts, a grim combat. Neither side possessed more reserves; each recognized the decisive phase. The raiders fought, Baker has it, with the recklessness of despera-

tion. The field resounded with the 'noise of horses, the cries of
wounded, the sound of horns'. Maupertuis teemed with individual
mêlées.

Medieval execution: the
executioner throws a
fit after a double
beheading

Then, abruptly, Buch's posse burst from concealment. The
effect on John's troops, especially the raw elements, of discovering
the enemy in its rear, predictably exceeded the scale of the intervention. Many fled in panic. The rest resisted fiercely as fortune
ebbed increasingly from their ranks. Scattered, finally, far across
the countryside, the battle concluded as a series of running fights

from which the French did their best to extricate themselves. For many, death or surrender were the only choices. John was among those who yielded their swords at last.

Even more than Crécy, Poitiers struck the times as an astonishing victory. Certainly, Anglo–Gascon losses, though not credibly quoted, were substantial. But the loss to France was much greater. An estimated 2,500 Frenchmen perished in the battle, including eight powerful magnates and almost 2,000 men-at-arms. As well as John, and his young son Philip, aged fourteen, twenty-six French lords of magnitude were captured, plus 1,933 lesser members of the chivalry.

Indeed, the number of prisoners was an immediate embarrassment. Unable to escort such a large group to Bordeaux, the captors paroled many on the spot under pledge to produce their ransoms later. For the Black Prince himself, only one captive mattered. In the King of France he held the key to profits beyond estimate.

Poitiers showed France responding, if uncertainly, to evolutionary pressures on the field of war. Compared with Crécy, it was a controlled and thoughtful battle on the French part which, had the Duke of Orleans remained to fight, must have given John victory.

Still, much understanding was lacking. The simple view of battle as a test of physical and moral prowess, exclusive of stratagems, died hard with the French warrior. With ample force for a flanking, even an encircling, movement, John had persisted in head-on engagement against a narrow, well defended front. With less resources, his enemies had supported their counter with a flanking stroke.

Again, while the French had regard for the lessons of earlier battles, these were misconstrued. The advantage of dismounted chivalry was in defensive, not offensive, engagement, as the Anglo–Gascon command recognized in the nature of its own attack. It is clear, also, that the importance of the archer's role, and the superiority of the longbow over the crossbow, had yet to be fully apprehended by the French.

As at Crécy, the sheer peril of the smaller force at Poitiers assured its inventiveness. The certainty that heroism alone could not suffice broke the spell of chivalric sentiment. There might be no glory in hiding along hedges, or in riding round woods to seek the foe's back, but survival not glory was the purpose of the

prince's troops. Two seasons of campaigning together had forged understanding and companionships. Harder won against a better organized enemy, the victory at Poitiers outclassed that of Crécy.

How far the Black Prince was personally its architect is debatable. His valour, as that of John, was unimpeachable. The chroniclers credit him with battlefield speeches which inspired his force. But in the actual disposal and tactics of the army it is easier to see the hand of such experienced leaders as Buch, Chandos and Audley (the last named, at least, until he fell wounded) than that of their flamboyant but less mature supremo. Indeed, the prince's own letters did not disguise the debt he owed his counsellors.

Finally, since it has become a convenience to think of the sides as French and English, it should be remembered that Poitiers was at least as much a struggle between Frenchmen and Frenchmen as between French and English troops. Gascons provided half or more of the prince's force. Theirs was the greatest knowledge of the land, its people, its martial proclivities; theirs the outstanding captain in the Captal of Buch. Poitiers confirmed the high renown of the Gascon as a fighting man.

Chapter 6

The French Revival

Installed after Poitiers in the manor of Savoy, between the City of London and Westminster, John was fêted and attended more as an ally than as a captive enemy. Indeed, no ally could have served the ambitions of Edward III so obligingly as his royal hostage served them in the few years left of his life.

Scrupulous in the details of courtly honour and ritual, the detained monarch respected the paroles and freedoms granted him. He had fought bravely. To the English nobles who met him socially, at jousts and various festivities, his good form in defeat was more important than his intellectual failings. Obsessed with mounting a great crusade, John exhorted his subjects to raise his ransom without delay.

France had problems enough without more expense. For a tax-ridden French population, in perpetual fear of raids and brigandry, Poitiers had been a knife twisted in its misery. In many places, burgesses and peasantry rose in revolt against the crown officers and overlords they blamed for their predicament. In Paris, the dauphin Charles, acting as regent, witnessed the murder of his closest friends before he fled the rioters.

Beauvais, Soissons and elsewhere erupted in an orgy of blood-shed as the long-suffering peasantry slaughtered nobles before wrecking their castles. To add to the chaos, Charles of Navarre escaped prison to rally his partisans against the crown. The revolts had scarcely been put down when John dropped a bomb-shell on the kingdom.

By treaty with Edward in London, the captive monarch agreed to a ransom so enormous, land concessions so sweeping, that the dauphin, having forced Charles of Navarre to terms at Pontoise, flatly refused to accept his father's settlement. Edward was furious.

In October 1359 the English king showed his displeasure by personally leading an expedition through northern France. From Calais, he devastated Artois, Thiérache and Champagne before being halted near Chartres, not by a French army, for none appeared, but by a violent storm. By now the dauphin's government was ready to negotiate. At last, with the French reduced to near impotence, there was a chance to end the war to the enduring advantage of the English crown. Characteristically, Edward ignored the long-term in the greed of the moment.

By the Peace of Brétigny, signed in May 1360, Edward re-claimed the whole duchy of Aquitaine as held by his ancestress

Opposite Bertrand Duguesclin, Constable of France

103

Queen Eleanor, the terms rejecting vassalage to the King of France. Despairingly, the dauphin's government sought to curtail the concessions of its captive king, but the settlement made was staggering. In addition to such counties as Poitou, the Limousin, Quercy, Marche and Angoumois, Edward retained Calais, acquired the northern district of Ponthieu, and imposed a sum of 3 million gold crowns as the price of John's ransom.

Perhaps only Edward could have imagined the successful transference of such power. The problem of controlling his new and largely unwilling subjects appears not to have daunted him.

As a wiser man must have realized, the circumstances of Valois humiliation were transitory. That the French kingdom, with far greater material resources than the kingdom of England, could long tolerate the results of such extortionate bargaining was, to say the least, improbable.

For the moment, however, Edward Plantagenet indulged his delusions of grandeur. John the Good had helped him to touch a dream. Though the French king had raised less than a third of his ransom when he died in London four years later, Edward held a brilliant funeral service for his former hostage at St Paul's, returning the body to Paris amid solemn pomp. On the face of it, John's successor, the youth who had consigned a third of France to England at Brétigny, seemed unlikely to give the English sovereign many sleepless nights.

Charles V of France was a sickly, emaciated prince, long of face and round-shouldered. Denied the powerful physique of his forbears, he combined a regal addiction to luxury with a fondness for art and instructive books. Exceptionally among the lords of the period, he actually read the contents of his library, ordering translations of classic works.

The military life did not appeal to King Charles. Eighteen years of age at Poitiers, he had witnessed that fateful day all the violence in which he wished personally to participate. At twenty-two, he became the first King of France to eschew direct command of the crown armies, and was perhaps the least warlike of all the French sovereigns.

But Charles was no shirker. Astute and patient, with a sharp, legalistic mind, the frail monarch applied himself committedly to redressing the ills which beset the kingdom when his father died. As his military lieutenant, he promoted Bertrand Duguesclin, a commoner as remarkable in his own way as the king himself.

Duguesclin was the antithesis of his royal master. Uncouth and formidably muscular, he had learned his warlike trade as an impoverished Breton knight amid the bands of pillaging men-at-arms which plagued the French countryside. The menace of the *routiers*, or 'free companies', had increased since the Treaty of Brétigny, which left thousands of mercenaries out of work.

When the Black Prince, newly created Prince of Aquitaine, barred them from his frontiers, they swarmed on the lands which remained to France, gravitating to the richest and least ravaged provinces. In bands a hundred or so strong, including Bretons, Gascons, Spaniards, a few English, and even German adventurers, the *routiers* terrorized every district they entered, seizing supplies as they wanted them, holding notables to ransom, ruining those who refused to buy protection. Some groups, by amalgamation, grew so powerful that they terrified large towns. The so-called *Tard-Venus*, or Latecomers, threatened Lyons. A union of companies formed in 1361 descended the Rhone, took Pont-Saint-Esprit and held the pope to ransom.

106   No one had the strength to destroy this human pestilence.

The crown lacked the money for a major campaign of extermination. Its great vassals were eluded, sometimes defeated, when they challenged the brigands. Local councils found it cheaper to buy off their tormenters than to pay for a regional defensive plan. Thus the evil was shifted from place to place.

Duguesclin's recommendation on entering Charles's service was no more than the notoriety of a *routier* captain. As such, his skills were in raiding and skirmishing, not in orthodox generalship. His first command in pitched battle, for the Count of Blois at Auray in the Breton war, resulted in his complete defeat and capture. But pitched battles were not on Charles V's mind. The king saw a use for the Breton's rugged talents.

The idea quite simply was to lure the *routiers* beyond France by directing their ambitions to foreign booty. Duguesclin, whose harsh authority and crude charm they recognized, was assigned the task. Initially, he suggested an eastern expedition against the Turks, but the *routiers* jibbed at the risk involved. Spain offered a tempting alternative. Here, the persecutions of Pedro the Cruel of Castile had driven his half-brother, Henry of Trastamare, into the arms of a rival sovereign, Pedro of Aragon. Trastamare and the King of Aragon were pleased to invite the *routiers* to join them in war against their enemy.

Accordingly, Duguesclin led the boldest of the 'free companies' across the Pyrenees, joined Trastamare on Spanish soil, and ousted his unpopular brother from Castile without trouble. But trouble was to follow, for Pedro the Cruel appealed for help to a source well positioned to effect his restitution, the Black Prince.

The victor of Poitiers was eager for new triumphs. When Pedro promised to foot the campaign bill, the Plantagenet headed promptly for Pamplona, where, leading an Anglo–Gascon army, he was soon making ground towards Duguesclin. Their meeting, near Nájera on the road from Vittoria, brought the Breton his second pitched battle and comprehensive beating. The prince's troops cut the enemy to pieces.

Ostensibly, the Spanish war, leaving a reinstated Castilian monarch indebted to the English, was a bonus for the buoyant Plantagenets. In fact it proved otherwise. For one thing, the Black Prince, stricken with fever in Spain, fell under the shadow of declining health. For another, Henry of Trastamare quickly settled the family feud by murdering his half-brother, leaving the prince's campaign expenses unpaid. These had now to be recouped in Aquitaine.

The effect of this was significant. By 1369 the taxes imposed on the newly annexed regions by the Black Prince had brought the people of western France close to rebellion. Charles V had cause to feel satisfied. The failure of Duguesclin's generalship at Nájera had eased the *routier* problem with ironic thoroughness. Like the Pied Piper of Hamelin, the swaggering Breton had led the miscreant companies to an abrupt end. Charles now had fresh work for him.

Despite the intervention of English and French forces in the wars of Spain and Brittany, the Treaty of Brétigny provided a nominal peace which lasted nine years. If it suited the ageing Edward, for Charles it was invaluable. The French monarch's need for time in which to rally his resources was clear in his efforts to keep the powers of London sweet. Payment of John's ransom was continued until more than half the sum agreed was paid.

Behind the conciliatory façade, the frail Valois prepared for the restoration of his kingdom. Militarily, two measures are notable. In 1367 an inquiry was initiated concerning the availability of archers throughout the land, and regular training was prescribed in each town. The same year, an inspection of castles was ordered to decide which were, or were not, effectively defensible. Those thought unlikely to be held were marked for destruction. The rest were to be kept repaired and garrisoned by the landlords, with financial assistance from royal funds.

Like many an unsoldierly man, Charles possessed a good strategic mind. From his father and grandfather he had learned the risks, not to say the expense, of the setpiece riposte to invasion. His own principles for war were evolving on special lines.

The main principle of defensive action was that no pitched battles should be fought. However eager his cavalry to avenge past defeats, it had to be restrained from mass engagement. Hostile armies should be met by withdrawal of the French behind stout walls, and by harassment of enemy communications and outposts where these were weakly held. Full advantage should be taken of opportunities for subversive activity within enemy-controlled towns and strongholds.

With the extension of Plantagenet rule over widespread areas of western France, the Valois forces at last possessed a real offensive choice. Hitherto, the lack of French bridgeheads in England, and the stout independence of the Gascons, had rendered Edward 108 relatively immune to invasion. With the huge territories of the

JOHANNES FILIVS QVARTVS
EDVARDI TERTII REX
CASTELLÆ ET LEGIONE
DVX LANCASTLIÆ
CONSTABVLARVS CASTE
DE QVEENSBOVRG QVIN
TO OCTOBRIS ANNO
REGNI EDW TERT EANN
GLIÆ 50 FRANCIÆ 37

HONI SOIT QVI MAL Y PENSE

110   John of Gaunt

Aquitanian principality to defend, he was as vulnerable to penetration as his rival. The sharpest answer to English raids, Charles perceived, was not confrontation on the field but retaliation in Aquitaine.

For such warfare, Duguesclin was well prepared. Limited objectives, surprise tactics, the exploitation of fear and disaffection to gain results: these were hall-marks of the 'free companies' the Breton had once led. He would impress them on the royal army.

The crown forces of France were not large, but they had improved in quality since John's day. Providently, the special taxes and administrative machinery implemented to raise John's ransom had been milked by Charles to provide war finances. Military pay was higher and more regular than before, while the iron authority which had enabled Duguesclin to impose his will among the *routiers* made for better discipline. Patiently, Charles awaited the time to act. It was signalled from the south-west.

Early in 1368, the estates of Aquitaine begrudgingly granted the Black Prince the taxes he needed to cover his Spanish expenses, but everywhere there was resentment. Appeals to the King of France, duly handled with much legalistic sophistry, led to Charles pronouncing his continuing sovereignty over Aquitaine. Conflict was inevitable.

Nevertheless, Charles refrained from actual warfare long enough to let Aquitanian discontent reach the boil. By way of encouraging rebellion against English rule, Charles's brother, the Duke of Anjou, issued bribes and promises liberally throughout the principality. Finally, in the summer of 1369, the King of France declared war against the Prince of Wales.

Edward III, entering his dotage, was no longer a personal force in the conflict. That year his queen, Philippa, died. Alice Perrers, the malign influence of his declining years, lay in wait for him. The Black Prince had become a chronic invalid.

Power in England was passing to John of Gaunt, Edward's fourth son, who had been Duke of Lancaster since 1362. Immensely rich through his first wife's inheritance, Gaunt was an earnest but uninspired warlord, committed to outdated martial policies. Doggedly, regardless of new boundaries and French methods, he pursued his father's old strategy of circular raids and devastations in northern France while Aquitaine crumbled, piece by piece, into Charles's lap. Five main English operations may briefly be mentioned.

The first of Gaunt's incursions, mounted from Calais late in 1369, involved a march to Harfleur and back through Artois and

Overleaf Siege fortifications (left) erected against a city (Brest)

111

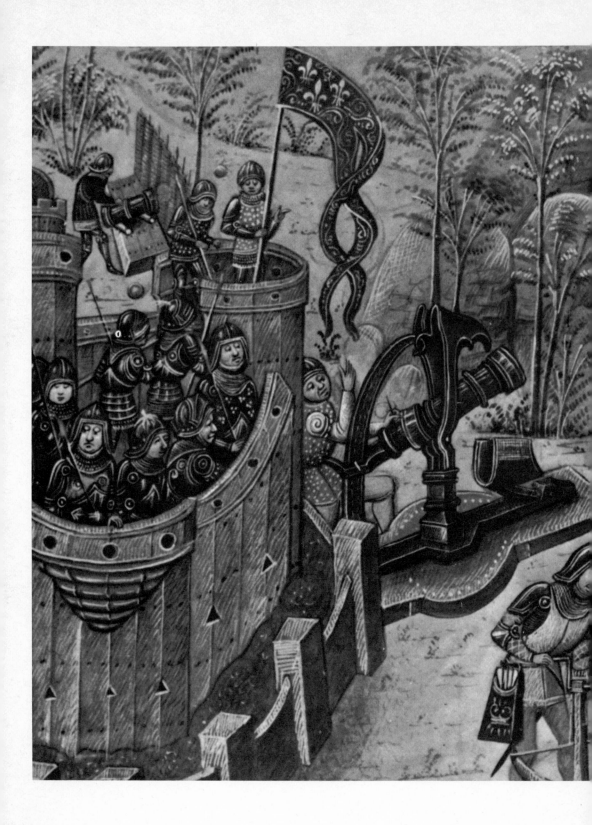

Picardy. The force was light; supplies were short. Charles disdained to be moved by it.

The following year, an English captain named Robert Knowles was entrusted with a fresh raid. Again, it started from Calais, inclining via Arras and Troyes towards Brittany. Unfortunately Knowles, though a soldier of high repute, was a commoner, lacking the ability to control the high-born noblemen in his force. The resulting discord provided Duguesclin with a fine chance. Pouncing as the quarrelsome English knights divided from their captain, the French commander scattered their isolated columns. The campaign ended with the annihilation of Knowles's rearguard near Le Mans.

The year 1373 saw Gaunt invading France for the second time. Determined to force an issue, the royal duke plunged deep into Charles's kingdom at the head of more than 10,000 men. Duguesclin, now Constable of France, was content to wait. When autumn arrived without offer of battle, Gaunt resolved to continue south and reinforce the English in Guienne. It was a rash plan. Winter, overtaking him in the central highlands, reduced his plight to desperation.

Everywhere strongholds and supplies were barred to his exhausted troops. Privation thinned the column; the French picked off the stragglers; hunger was remorseless. It was almost Christmas when Gaunt descended to the plain of the Dordogne and approached Bordeaux. He had lost half his army by the wayside.

This hapless enterprise was followed by two equally fruitless raids, the last during Edward's reign. In 1375 Edmund, Earl of Cambridge, marched Brittany from end to end, and the Earl of Buckingham later duplicated Knowles's advance into Maine, continuing as far as Rennes.

Meanwhile, the French in the south had been making dramatic gains. By a combination of diplomatic coups and well chosen sieges, Duguesclin and the Duke of Anjou recovered territory after territory at little loss to themselves. In a triumphant campaign during 1370, all Agenais and most of Limousin submitted to the French crown. Beyond the Garonne, Bazas acknowledged Charles.

Two years later, the French swept toward Poitou and Saintonge. La Rochelle surrendered in September. English reinforcements had been overwhelmed at sea by a fleet provided by Henry of Trastamare. On land and water alike, Plantagenet hopes sank. By spring 1374 French troops were at La Réole, a day's march from Bordeaux. In less than five years, all the lands annexed under

the Treaty of Brétigny had been won back to Charles's fold,

and what remained of Plantagenet Guienne was in serious danger. Furthermore, Abbeville and Ponthieu in the north had been reclaimed.

At a time when the forces of his kingdom were far from overwhelming, the unsoldierly Charles had engineered a reversal of fortunes that questioned some of the most cherished military procedures of the war to date.

The 'war ride', the great raid of devastation on which the English had pinned their faith, was exposed at last as a strategic failure. Equally challenged was the concept of setpiece combat. If Crécy and Poitiers had not destroyed the belief of many knights and captains in the mounted charge, there was now no denying that sweeping gains could be achieved without recourse to pitched battle. And above all, the Duguesclin war, as it is sometimes called, witnessed a general retreat from those aspects of armed conflict perhaps best defined as chivalric.

For the first time in the war, the French had devised a system of campaigning based on realism rather than the maintenance of knightly glory and self-esteem. Under orders not always pleasing to their vanity, French captains shut themselves safely in citadels bristling with the newly skilled bowmen of the communes and fought only when the outcome was beyond doubt. They used stratagems. They took advantage of fraud and treachery. In short, they began to treat war as a calculated business, not merely a dashing sport for gentlemen. The success of the new approach hushed its critics and discouraged the humanitarian spirit which enlightened the better side of chivalry. The merciless atrocities later witnessed in the Wars of the Roses and the feud between Orleans and Burgundy were presaged by the trends of Duguesclin's day.

Neither the panegyric of Duguesclin's biographer Cuvelier, nor the puffs of the prolific versifier Christine de Pisan, could hide his unscrupulous methods and temperament. The war of the 1370s brought out the worst in its protagonists. The Black Prince was no exception. Carried on a litter, the ailing lord wrought bitter vengeance on his deserting subjects in Aquitaine.

At the sack of Limoges in 1370, a punishment for the city's pro-French activities, the prince ordered the slaughter of hundreds of inhabitants. Even those chroniclers accustomed to glossing over war's inhumantities expressed shock. 'There is none with so hard a heart that he would not have wept in pity at the great cruelty,' wrote Froissart. 'May God preserve the souls of the men, women and children massacred that day. They were martyrs.'

By the middle of the decade, a growing war-weariness led to the first of a series of truces preceding a longer peace. The initial armistice, made at Bruges in 1375, endured until 1377, when both the Black Prince and his father died. After all his strivings and triumphs, Edward III had lived to see his grand illusions shattered, the English dominion in France shrunk to Calais and a foothold between Bordeaux and Bayonne.

Three years later, Charles of France and Duguesclin died. On both sides of the Channel problems of domestic politics took precedence over military enterprise. In England the succession of Richard II, the ten-year-old son of the Black Prince, left the realm not only enfeebled but intransigent. In France Charles VI, twelve when his father died, was oppressed, as was Richard, by scheming relatives.

Neither kingdom had its heart in continued war; each was reluctant to settle for permanent peace as positions stood. In 1380, the English, still smarting from their losses in southern France, mounted a final raid from Calais under Thomas of Woodstock,

116

Edward III's youngest son. For their own part, the French looked to an invasion of England as the logical sequel to the successes of Charles V.

During the summer of 1385, and again a year later, ships, men and materials were concentrated at the Norman ports while the Scots prepared for a simultaneous assault on Richard's kingdom. In England the threat was viewed with intense dismay. But the danger passed with curious passivity. For reasons now obscure, the French armada never put to sea. It was as if France, without the wit and vision of Charles V, had lost the will to sustain her new-style martial effort.

Reaction flowed into the armed ranks. Knights, accustomed to sole proprietorship of the limelight, objected to the raised status of bowmen. Captains hankered for their time-honoured tactics. Bored by Duguesclin's prosaic ghost, the chivalry of France turned back to its old romantic image.

Meanwhile, negotiations between the kingdoms dragged on. Desultory fighting gave way to longer truces. Finally, in 1396, the two kings, youth effaced in the wrangling, concluded the so-called Peace of Paris.

Technically, this odd agreement was another truce on the basis of the status quo. As such, it saved Richard the humiliation of renouncing a vain title to the French dominion he had never held. However, since the truce was arranged for thirty years, and survived for almost twenty, it perhaps deserves its elevation to the form of a peace. The sword was sheathed – until a new generation drew it again.

Chapter 7

Sea Raids, Radicals and Lancastrians

Campaign after campaign ruthlessly aimed at the ruin and terrorization of civilians ensured that the chief victims of the Hundred Years War were not soldiers but non-combatants. Generally the people of France had the worst of it, but English coastal communities also suffered very badly. Sea raids were numerous and unmerciful.

From the earliest days of the conflict, the south shore of England was a target for amphibious assaults of varying strength and penetration. Portsmouth and Southampton were sacked on more than one occasion; fishing hamlets were burned from Thanet west to Plymouth. Further afield, the Channel Islands, loyal to England, were attacked repeatedly, Guernsey succumbing to French occupation for seven years from 1338.

Neither dominance at sea, which was England's for a period after Sluys, nor the capture of Calais, which gave Edward a pincer-grip on the adjacent straits, stopped French raiding. Sea command, in the modern sense of exclusivity, was beyond the scope of admirals whose forces were clumsy, scattered and too often in the thrall of perverse winds.

Regular naval forces were never great, and as time reduced funds the kings had to sell their ships. At its highpoint of the fourteenth century, the royal navy of France possessed perhaps forty craft, fifty at the outside, but by 1384 it had dwindled to a handful of old, decrepit galleys. Richard II had four royal vessels; Henry IV, half a dozen.

Both sides resorted, in consequence, to foreign fleets, particularly Spanish and Genoese mercenaries. Again, this was expensive. The hire of eleven Genoese vessels for a short season in 1373 cost England £9,550. But, as raiders, the southern fleets gave value, their shallow-draught oar-and-sail-propelled galleys being ideal for inshore work. Much destruction on the English coast was inflicted by Castilians.

In August 1350, the Plantagenet fleet achieved a rare interception off Winchelsea. A Castilian freebooter, Carlos de la Cerda, had sailed north under contract to France and based his ships in Flanders. On the way he had captured several English vessels and put their crews to death. Edward III planned to ambush the Spaniards in the Channel.

It was an ambitious project. The time needed to assemble 'arrested' vessels, impress mariners, and await favourable winds before moving to desired points had much to do with the low incidence of sea-to-sea engagements at the period. Raiding

Opposite Naval attack on St Michel

119

squadrons had little to fear from interception. Indeed, despite Edward's exceptional efforts, Cerda almost certainly could have avoided action had he so wished, but clearly he did not.

On the afternoon of 29 August, the Spaniards were sighted from Winchelsea running down the Channel before a north-easterly to the strength of about forty sail. Edward had been waiting most of the month at the little port with some fifty vessels, including his flagship the *Thomas*. With him were the Black Prince and Henry of Lancaster. As they put out from Winchelsea, Cerda, with time to slip past, instead steered straight at them.

In part, the Castilian's confidence reposed in the superior size and build of his craft, whose upper works towered over the English decks. There was assurance, too, in the powerful arms he had shipped in Flanders at French expense. In addition to the Spanish bowmen who had sailed north with him, Cerda had packed his fleet with tough Flemish mercenaries.

The action, known in history as Les Espagnols-sur-Mer, commenced with near disaster for Edward. At the moment of engagement, the cog *Thomas*, colliding with the foremost of the Spanish ships, was holed and began to sink. Luckily for the king, his crew managed to grapple another enemy, and to capture and transfer to her. Later the Prince of Wales boarded a Spaniard as his own craft wallowed dangerously.

It was a costly fight. Crossbow fire from the Castilians was withering, but the larger number of English vessels, and the deeper motivation of their warriors, at length prevailed over the profit-conscious mercenaries. Hope of rich prizes had led Cerda into battle. As hope dwindled, so did the Spanish fleet. One coup of outstanding note had eluded it.

The ship carrying Edward's household, commanded by Robert Namur, had been grappled and placed in tow when a squire in Namur's service contrived to board the captor and bring down her sail by cutting its halyards and stays with his sword. Losing way, the Spaniard was herself captured.

By dusk, the marauders had drawn off, leaving about a third of their vessels in Edward's hands. Though the king's men had suffered heavy casualties, in craft they were actually better off. Winchelsea had reinforced the verdict of Sluys on the ruggedness of the English battle fleet.

With reason, Charles V gave his navy a lot of thought. In its main dockyard, the Clos des Galées at Rouen, France possessed an establishment unequalled in England. Charles made it work for him. New galleys were commissioned; existing ships were overhauled. Private vessels were bought by the government. Harfleur and Dieppe were established as naval depots. While Duguesclin took command of the army, Charles appointed an equally unorthodox admiral for his navy in John of Vienne, a landsman whose interest in the sea was largely theoretical. He seems never to have gone on it of free choice. Vienne was soon planning fresh assaults on the English coast.

At Harfleur in 1377, he reviewed a grand fleet of about fifty ships, with several thousand troops aboard, assigned to devastate the Channel ports. Sailing in late June, the force quickly took Rye, then unwalled, and thrust inland to Lewes. The townsmen, led by the prior, were defeated and their homes burned. Winchelsea, hastily garrisoned by the Abbot of Battle, escaped attack as the French regained the sea and sailed west.

Plymouth was next sacked and left in flames. In August the raiders overwhelmed and pillaged the Isle of Wight, but by this time much of the coast had been reinforced and they failed to take Poole and Southampton, the latter ably defended by Sir John Arundel. With the southern shires under full alert, Vienne's armada made a last call at Hastings, reducing the town to ashes before returning to the shores of France.

Such terror brought the war, and its ruin, home to many unwarlike Englishmen, thus aggravating the rising swell of social discontent. Men who enlisted to enrich themselves by robbing and looting stood a fair chance of doing so. Those who paid through taxation for the raising and deployment of armies, it seemed, had their homes razed. They expected protection for their money. As the people of France had shown by the riots after Poitiers, vain sacrifice was an inflammatory formula.

By the 1370s, the war was being questioned widely. As the country and Parliament persistently queried costs, government propaganda became a necessary tool against scepticism about, even downright opposition to, military policies. Letters and pictures were employed, and the Church was enlisted to arouse enthusiasm for campaigns and denounce the king's foes as common enemies.

But not all churchmen took to their pulpits in the cause of war. Apart from efforts by the papacy in the diplomatic field, individual clerics on both sides spoke out against the conduct of the conflict, sometimes against war itself. Thomas Brinton, Bishop of Rochester, was among those who held that God disapproved of the war with 121

France. Charles's victories in Aquitaine were, he said, a divine retribution on England for taking part. The persecution of non-combatants aroused special indignation, and means of preventing it were discussed.

In France, such commentators on military conduct as the fourteenth-century priest Honoré Bonet and his contemporary Philippe de Mézières, the soldier and author, readily put a finger on the need for the better payment of armies. Properly paid troops would not need to pillage, they argued, and could be disciplined. Doubtless, few commanders would have disagreed. But where the money might be found was another thing.

Among those who attacked not just the methods and objectives of armies but all forms of armed aggression, John Wycliffe was pre-eminent. Wycliffe, who died shortly before the Peace of Paris, condemned warfare as unchristian, castigating crown and clergy for espousing it. Warlike policies, he averred, were pursued 'for pride and coveitise'. Bluntly, Wycliffe challenged the right of any prince to risk the lives of his people on the assumption that his claim to a disputed kingdom was backed by God.

After Wycliffe's death, Walter Brut and William Swynderby, among other Englishmen, continued to denounce war. That they were taken seriously is evidenced by the fact that the theological establishment of Cambridge felt obliged to defend the King of England's right to attack France.

Other issues were smouldering. Exacerbated by war and the economics of the Black Death, a profound mood of radicalism disturbed the land. Everywhere rising wages, bringing higher expectations into conflict with feudal law, encouraged restlessness. 'The world goeth fast from bad to worse,' wrote John Gower, an English country gentleman.

> Labourers of old were not wont to eat of wheaten bread; their meat was of beans or coarse corn, and their drink of water alone. Cheese and milk were a feast to them, and rarely ate they of other dainties ... Age, whither turnest thou? for now the poor demand to be better fed than their masters. Moreover, they bedeck themselves in fine attire whereas they would be clad in sackcloth as of old.

But neither Gower, nor anyone else, could turn back the clock. Protest against injustice was gaining voice. Wycliffe advocated the equality of bondsmen and gentry. John Ball, a York priest who moved to Essex, preached reform despite repeated arraignment by the Canterbury primate. His message was summarized by Froissart in these words:

Wat Tyler (standing
left) with John Ball
(mounted)

My good friends, matters cannot be well in England until all things
shall be in common; when there shall be neither vassals nor lords;
when the lords shall no more be the masters than ourselves. How ill
they treat us ! By what justification do they hold us thus in bondage ?
Are we not all descended from the same parents, Adam and Eve ?
And what can they show, what reason give, why they should be
masters ?

They wear velvet and rich stuffs, ornamented with ermine and other
furs, while we are obliged to wear poor clothing. They have wines,
spices and fine bread, while we have only rye and straw refuse. They
have handsome seats and manors, while we must brave the wind
and rain in our labours ... and it is by our labour they are able to
support their pomp.

Four years after Richard II's accession, war measures brought
discontent to a head in the abrupt and confused risings known as

the Peasants' Revolt. The immediate cause of the disturbances was a government move against the widespread evasion of a general war tax.

The worst troubles occurred in those regions picked for special investigation; that is, in the shires of the south-east and a number of isolated areas as far removed as the Wirral and Yorkshire. Like the French risings of the period, it was a movement of both town and countryside, seemingly spontaneous and lacking general leadership.

Peasants and artisans, disgruntled clerics, the poor and the not so poor – suddenly a great mass of people had joined together against the men of influence: manorial lords, wealthy merchants, war leaders such as John of Gaunt, ecclesiastical dignitaries of disrepute.

London saw the most serious tumult. On 13 June 1381 the demonstrators of Kent and Essex, led by Wat Tyler of Maidstone and John Ball, entered the city in their thousands and made cause with local elements. There was much promiscuous violence. John's old lodging, the Savoy, a Gaunt property, was burned down. The Hospital of St John of Jerusalem, near Smithfield, was levelled. Aliens, particularly Flemings, were massacred. 'Hardly was there a street in which there were not bodies of the slain,' records one account.

> The whole of the infuriated rout took its way towards the Tower of London, entering which by force they dragged forth Sir Simon Sudbury, the Archbishop of Canterbury, Chancellor of our Lord the King, and Brother Robert Hales, Prior of the Hospital of St John of Jerusalem, the King's Treasurer, and, together with them Brother William Appletone of the Order of Friars Minor, and John Leg, Sergeant at Arms to the King, and also one Richard Somenour of the Parish of Stepney; all of whom they beheaded in the place called Tower Hill; and then they set their heads up on London Bridge.

Taken by surprise, the young king and his advisers desperately played for time. By an astute combination of prevarication and appeasement, Richard retrieved the situation with amazing speed. By the 15th, when he met the crowd at Smithfield, he had the backing of a substantial force of armed citizens, collected by the mayor, William Walworth. Despite a scrimmage between Walworth and Tyler, in which the latter was wounded, the rebels dispersed on the acceptance of a number of their demands, including the abolition of villeinage.

Beyond London, the demonstrations were fairly easily suppressed by the authorities. Many ringleaders paid a severe penalty. Tyler

124

was dragged from St Bartholomew's Hospital and beheaded. Ball was hanged, drawn and quartered in the king's presence and his remains exhibited in four towns.

If reaction to the Peasants' Revolt was less savage than the suppressions visited on similar Continental movements, bitterness lingered. In 1399, a Wycliffite rising provoked repression of the fiercest kind. A contemporary chronicler, Adam of Usk, put the number slaughtered at 23,000. For much of England, the evils of radicalism, whether of the Tyler or the related Wycliffe variety, were scarcely less absorbing than the war with France.

Richard, having declared himself of age in 1389, ruled as a constitutional monarch until the Peace of Paris, when, marrying Isabella, daughter of Charles VI, he appears suddenly to have adopted French tastes and manners and to have asserted absolutist pretensions.

A tall man with a soft white face, thin moustaches and the double-pointed beard of the period, he looks in his portraits both effeminate and villainous. His enemies did not doubt the second attribute. In the last three years of his reign he banished the Earl of Warwick, the Archbishop of Canterbury and the Dukes of Norfolk and Hereford, beheaded the Earl of Arundel and imprisoned the Duke of Gloucester (who died in prison, probably murdered).

Having thus provoked the opprobrium of powerful interests, he was perhaps unwise in 1399 to leave the country for Ireland, allowing his cousin Henry Bolingbroke, the son of John of Gaunt, to prepare an austere homecoming for him. Richard's own incarceration and mysterious death struck a not unfamiliar note. The accession of Henry IV, first of the Lancastrian monarchs, disposed of the old century with an awkward twist to Anglo–French relationships.

Opposite Richard II of England

But if Charles VI resented the fate of his son-in-law, civil strife between Orleans and Burgundy exercised him more. John, Duke of Burgundy, holding vast tracts in northern France and the Low Countries, had quarrelled violently with his cousin Louis, Duke of Orleans, the king's brother, whose power was in central and southern France.

Occasionally, one or other party transgressed the Peace of Paris. In 1403, an Orleanist admiral raided Plymouth and other Channel ports. Three years later, the Burgundians joined their rivals in a futile attempt on Guienne and Calais, but co-operation

126

RICARDVS   II

128   Richard II entertaining the dukes in London

was short-lived. Soon afterwards, the Duke of Orleans was murdered by agents of Burgundy and uncompromising civil war gripped France.

Indeed the formal truce between kingdoms suited both crowns. Henry IV, constantly hampered by lack of money – and, in his later years, by ill health – had domestic problems of his own. The Scots and Owen Glendower, the Welsh rebel, were troublesome. The great families of England perpetuated the ferment of Richard's reign. Their lesser neighbours clamoured and plotted. Luckily for Henry, not an easily daunted man, the opposition failed to make common cause. In 1411 and 1412, by way of repaying Continental scores, he loaned troops to the Burgundians and Orleanists respectively.

Charles of France, now middle-aged, was a tragic prince. While feuding factions tore his realm apart, and a coarse wife, Isabella of Bavaria, flaunted her lovers in his weary face, the latest Valois king lapsed into spells of insanity, convinced he was made of glass and might disintegrate. And as a symbol of French vulnerability, the delusion was apt enough. Sooner or later, the fullness of England's opportunity had to dawn on her aggressive lords – and one already had an eye on the main chance.

While Henry IV sank towards his death in 1413, his son, Henry of Monmouth, prepared eagerly for his hour of power. No leader could have risen in England at that moment with greater menace for a tortured France. A man of precocious martial ability, he had commanded English forces at the age of sixteen against the rebel Percies, defeating them at Shrewsbury. By twenty he was a veteran, his talents proved against the Welsh revolt.

Romance and the genius of Shakespeare have distorted the image of Henry V, but his puissance is clear and thrilled society from the first. Apart from military victories, he gave England two things rare in the late Middle Ages, a strong leader and positive government. In the nine years he was to reign before his early death at thirty-five, Henry was to raise the influence of his kingdom to paramouncy in Christendom.

But he was no romantic hero. Long-nosed and lantern-jawed, his head shaved to leave an island of hair on a high skull, Henry affected a style of formal piety scarcely embellished by his other traits, among which were cruelty, cunning and covetousness. Harsh to his subjects, he was pitiless to his enemies. Politically, he was quite unscrupulous. Like Edward III, he married improvidence with overweening ambition in foreign enterprise, a field in which his policies ultimately proved as short-sighted as Edward's. 129

130   Henry IV of England

From the onset of his reign, Henry was determined to attack France, calculating not only to exploit her own troubles but also thereby to divert the unruly vigour of his nobles to another land. As a preliminary, he revived the claims of his ancestors. Aquitaine should be returned to him. He demanded the long forgotten arrears of King John's ransom. He even asked for the hand of one of Charles's daughters, with a suitable dowry.

The demands increased with each embassy. Soon the price asked of Orleanists and Burgundians alike for Henry's friendship was far beyond what the Treaty of Brétigny had cost France. Neither faction would accept such terms. Nor had Henry expected that they would. In the course of negotiations, he had steadily advanced his invasion plans, raising and equipping a force of 12,000 troops. By the spring of 1415 he was ready. That April he declared war.

Chapter 8

Harfleur and Agincourt

For the first time in the memory of most men, a king of England was venturing on France again. The lords who followed him – his brothers the Dukes of Clarence and Gloucester; his cousin the Duke of York, and his uncle the Earl of Dorset; the Earls of March, Suffolk, Arundel and others; the Bishops of Norwich and Bangor; and nineteen fighting barons – vied in the brilliance of their panoply.

Armour had not changed greatly since their forbears fought with Edward III. Plate had mostly taken the place of mail, which remained to protect the neck between helmet and body plates, otherwise knights wore the same all-embracing shell, impossible to don without help, restrictive of agility.

The lavish style of the fourteenth century, the splendid *côte d'armes* and the ornamented sword belt, still flourished in the fifteenth. Nobles still embarked for war with retinues of pages, grooms, chaplains and squires; still clung to the outward modes of chivalry. But a new stress on practicalities appeared in Henry's force.

It was seen in the king's resolve to pay his troops punctually and regularly. Scales of remuneration were fixed at the outset. Dukes were to receive 13s. 4d. a day, earls 6s. 8d., barons 4s., knights 2s., other men-at-arms 1s., archers 6d. Since the expedition included about 2,000 knights and men-at-arms, and some 8,000 archers, not to mention the host of seamen and non-combatants mustered in its support, the bill was a large one. Indeed Henry pawned his crown jewels to provide collateral for the campaign.

Tradesmen and technicians littered the payroll. Apart from the customary armourers, fletchers, bowyers, carpenters, farriers, wheelwrights, and so on, there was a marked emphasis on siege specialists. The force included 120 miners and seventy-five artillerists trained in the new art of cannonry.

Since the invention of the cannon in the early fourteenth century, crude forms of the weapon had been tested in European engagements without impressing many commanders. It was not until the fifteenth century, when cast barrels of some sophistication appeared, that gunpowder propulsion began to replace the catapult principle in artillery.

Opposite Henry V of England

Though Henry regarded cannons as important siege weapons, they were not popular with troops of the period. Like the tactical refinement of archery, the introduction of the cannon threatened the knight's status, lending weight to those by no means thought of as gentlemen. Many gunners were not even soldiers, but civilian

engineers with a taste for living dangerously. The powder of the day, still mixed in the field, was as likely to blow the guns as their targets to pieces. Its fulminations imparted a Mephistophelean aura to the medieval gunner. He was feared and shunned by other men.

Henry of Monmouth was a thorough commander. A body of surgeons had been assembled for the campaign. Herds of cattle were embarked to provide meat on the hoof as the force advanced. Spares of all kinds were prominent on the supply lists. Finally, every captain was given a copy of thirty-four war ordinances governing troop behaviour, and instructed to inform his men accordingly.

The armada was gathered on the Hampshire coast, facing the Isle of Wight. At Spithead lay the *Trinity Royal*, Henry's flagship, her top-castle surmounted with a crown of gleaming copper gilt while a gold-painted leopard carved in wood adorned her deck-head. With a crew of 300 and 500 tons portage, she was the largest of the royal craft.

Ships of all sizes from twenty tons upwards lay to either side. Every available transport had been impressed. So tightly was the fleet packed that when one vessel caught fire the flames spread to two others. All three were immobilized. The incident was seen by many as an evil sign. Luckily for morale, a flock of swans appeared soon afterwards. The omens were good again. On 11 August, a Sunday, the fleet slipped into the Channel and headed south.

Had it been possible for the French to miss the English preparation, they could hardly have misconstrued Henry's sentiments. His destiny, he proclaimed, was to restore the fortunes of France by taking charge of them. Defensive measures against him were complicated by rivalries. An uncertain peace agreed between Orleanists and Burgundians in February had left the dual roles of moderator and defence chief in the youthful hands of the dauphin, Charles of Ponthieu, a less than dynamic prince.

Opposite Charles VI of France

The immediate task of raising troops fell on the Constable of France, Charles d'Albret. At his side was the redoubtable marshal, Boucicaut, alias Jean le Meingre, a warrior renowned for distant victories against the Turks and for founding a society to protect the womenfolk of absent knights (the *Dame blanche à l'ecu vert*).

Hindered by lack of response from the Burgundians, and doubts as to where the English might land, Albret made Rouen his point of muster while Boucicaut watched the coast at Honfleur. Their positioning was pretty good. On the afternoon of 14 August

Henry's fleet dropped anchor at Chef de Caux, on the north shore of the Seine estuary, a few miles across the water from Honfleur.

His objective was the more prominent Norman port of Harfleur. The temptation to back his claim to Aquitaine by direct assault in the south had not inveigled him. Over-extended lines had proved disastrous to Edward in Duguesclin's day. Henry opted for short communications.

Harfleur, commanding the Seine mouth (Le Havre did not then exist), was among the most important bases on the French coast, at once handy to England and the gateway to Normandy. Having obtained such a vital port, the English might move east towards the Somme, pursuing the Seine towards Paris or pushing south to the heart of Charles's kingdom.

Henry's strategy differed radically from that of Edward and John of Gaunt. Instead of destructive but futile raids, the new challenger had set before himself the methodical task of conquering France in detail, bastion by bastion, town by town. But first Harfleur had to be taken.

This was no easy task. Though the garrison, under the Lord of Estouteville, was not numerous, the fortifications were considerable. The town possessed a strong wall with more than two dozen guard towers and a wet moat. Moreover, the approaches were extensively covered by marshy ground. The defenders had made the most of their advantages. Bridges had been destroyed, streams dammed to flood the countryside. Heavy timber barbicans reinforced the town gates. From the ramparts, crossbowmen and artillerists scanned all avenues, while quicklime and hot oil stood at readiness.

Altogether, the town illustrated pretty much the type of obstacle fourteenth-century raiders had preferred to skirt with a side-glance. Henry's hopes of success rested heavily on artillery.

Precise details of the weapons available to him are not known. A report reaching Paris gave the number of English heavy cannons as a dozen, of which the largest were twelve feet in length and over two feet in calibre. Three at least had nicknames: the London, the Messenger and the King's Daughter. Erupting in dense clouds of black smoke, these monsters hurled projectiles weighing up to 500 lbs, including complete millstones. Their capacity to demolish masonry was substantial, though the need to place them near enough to their targets for accuracy added to the hazards of the gunners.

Gun teams were exposed to fire from the French towers as they moved up, crouched behind wooden screens. Groups of men-at-

The marriage of Henry V and Catherine of Valois

137

arms sallied from the town to attack the artillerists. Nevertheless, the guns did persuasive work. For a week their barrage was continuous, pounding not only the walls but also the town within.

French attempts to effect repairs under cover of darkness were discouraged by night bombardment. Timber works were destroyed by gun stones soaked in tar and set alight before firing. The result, a significant curtailment of Harfleur's will and ability to resist siege, was a triumph for the latest addition to martial science. Henry ordered more guns.

The investment of Harfleur, though less than six weeks old when the town surrendered in September, was still of sufficient duration to demonstrate the dangers of static war to a medieval field force. Three main problems taxed the English king.

Food shortages emerged as army requirements exhausted local reserves and the land's supplies. Disorder and disruption occurred as a result of inactivity among the bulk of the troops, and the frustration of their aggressive impulse. And, finally, disease arose from the insanitary conditions of camp life and bad diet.

Henry dealt adequately with the first of these difficulties. Much space on the ships had been given to provisions, and various supporting arrangements had been put in hand. For instance, men from the Cinque Ports had been directed to fish off the Norman coast and unload their catches for the army. Shellfish, prolific in the creeks around Harfleur, were collected by the soldiers.

With the second problem, Henry coped superbly. Discipline was uniquely good. For the first time in the war an English army had come to France not bent unashamedly on a policy of devastation but, at least ostensibly, to restore peace and order to that country. The king did not intend to be discredited by his troops. Nor, it is clear, did he underestimate the correlation between military efficiency and orderliness.

The weeks of siege were a stiff challenge. Boredom raised familiar difficulties. Englishmen, Welshmen and Irishmen, mingled with groups of foreign mercenaries, represented an explosive mix only too ready to erupt in unauthorized sorties and camp brawls.

One source of trouble, the prostitutes attracted by troop concentrations, was eliminated by an order forbidding their approach on pain of having their limbs broken. 'It was considered a crime to have bad women in the camp,' wrote a chronicler. It was also a crime to obtain unofficial transport by taking carts and beasts of

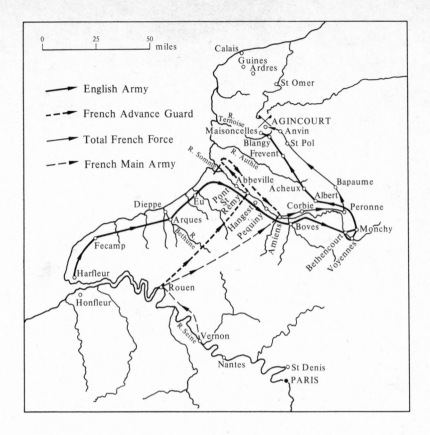

The Agincourt Campaign

burden from the locals. To distinguish soldiers from civilian miscreants, the former were compelled to display red St George's crosses on the backs and fronts of their tunics. Far from all the regulations were new, but the vigour of their enforcement was original. As the French monk of St Denys admitted, the king was 'obeyed scrupulously'. Rape and the murder of women, together with the plundering of churches, were capital offences; abuse of the sacrament was punishable by hanging, drawing and quartering. Pillaging and freebooting were also subject to heavy penalties.

In the area of health, however, even Henry's powers were circumscribed. The insanitary conditions common to medieval field camps, aggravated by unusually hot weather that summer, brought a wave of illness on the army. Dietary irregularities did not help. Apart from shellfish, an abundance of unripe fruit was consumed. Within weeks, dysentery had reached epidemic proportions.

Overleaf Fifteenth-century siege showing a variety of fortifications and weapons

139

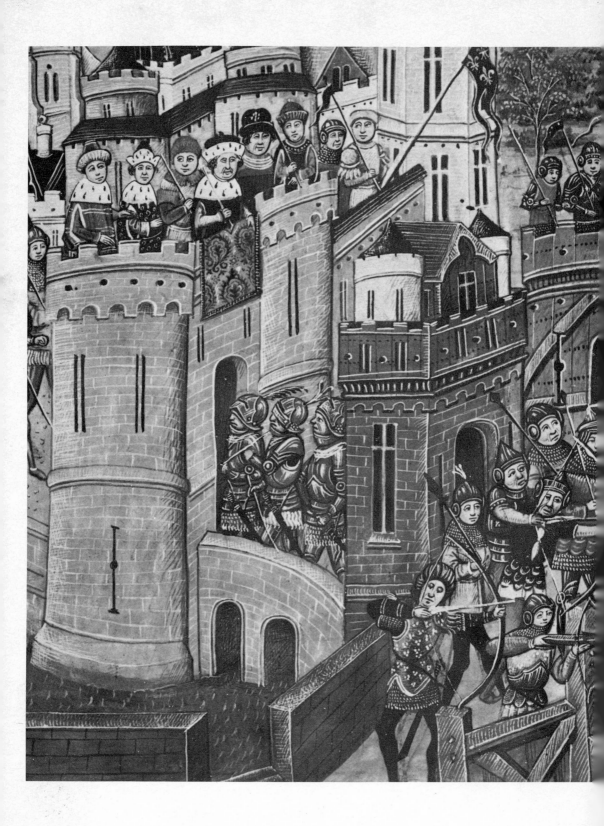

Among the first to die was the Bishop of Norwich, Richard Courtenay, a close adviser of the king. Soon, the Duke of Clarence and Earls of Suffolk, March and Arundel were lying ill. Hundreds of the lower ranks perished or were shipped home as invalids. Indeed, by the time Harfleur was firmly in Henry's hands, his army had dwindled to less than 8,000 men. It must have seemed to the captains a perverse irony that an operation so efficiently mounted and successful in its first aim should have fallen into such straits. Clearly, Henry's planned campaign of conquest was ruled out. With a garrison of 2,000 assigned to the captured port, something like 900 men-at-arms and 5,000 other troops, mostly archers, remained for further operations. Of this modest force, a disconcerting portion was enfeebled by poor health.

On 5 October a council of Henry's commanders and great lords produced two well supported proposals: one, for the withdrawal of all save the garrison to England; the other, for limiting expansion to an enclave around the town.

The king argued with passion for a bolder course. His motives were plain enough. After all the proclamations and expenses of the past months, an aborted campaign must greatly weaken his standing in England. The thought of handing such a gift to his political opponents was a bitter one. If he could not proceed as intended, at least he had to save face. Accordingly, Henry mooted an advance north to Calais – a brisk march away from likely trouble, yet spanning enough of France to rescue his pretensions from ridicule.

True, it involved risk, but he seemed safe in counting on French disunity. Charles VI and the dauphin were moving slowly down the Seine from Paris calling the kingdom to service. Response was proving tardy. The Duke of Burgundy offered no more than promises. The Orleanists, fearing their rival would enter Paris if they joined the royal host, were uncooperative. The people as a whole fretted more over taxes than Harfleur. At Rouen, Albret had assembled a fair force but appeared ready to wait until the main body joined him.

Geographically, the situation favoured Henry's project. The gathering under Charles and the dauphin was at Vernon, a river town as far from Calais as was Harfleur. Travelling light, and with a flying start, the English should have little difficulty keeping ahead of the main French host which, in any case, was not complete.

Rouen was a day's march nearer Calais than Harfleur; Albret better prepared than his masters. But again the advantage of surprise was with Henry. Albret must lose a day receiving news of a departure and making way. Even assuming he achieved an interception, it was improbable he would attack until reinforced.

The plan Henry put to his council envisaged an advance by the quickest possible route to Calais, where the army could then enship for England. Holding close to the coast, he would ford the Somme near Abbeville, at the throat of the estuary, as had Edward III prior to Crécy. Food would be carried to save the need for foraging, otherwise impedimenta would be cut to the minimum.

Persisting doubts among his nobles were countered, it seems, by a stirring speech. Henry's fifteenth-century biographer, Tito Livio, told how the king spoke of a 'burning desire' to traverse the territories he claimed. If the gesture were not made, the French would be contemptuous.

> They would say that through fear I have fled away acknowledging the injustice of my cause. But I have a mind my brave men to encounter all dangers rather than let them brand your king with ill words. By the favour of God we will go unhurt and inviolate, and, if they attempt to stop us, victorious and triumphant in all glory.

A week into October, the English army set out.

The weather was still fine. Carved animals, painted in blue and gold, glistened atop the towers of Harfleur. The column headed for Arques by way of Fécamp.

It proceeded in three parts: the vanguard commanded by the respected knights Sir John Cornwall and Sir Gilbert Umfraville; the main body with the king, his brother Gloucester and John Holland (later Earl of Huntingdon, a young captain whose dash during the siege had caught Henry's eye); and the rearguard under York and the Earl of Oxford.

Travelling 'light' was a qualified exercise. Though the ordinary soldiers carried little but their weapons and rations, the bulky armour of the chivalry had to be transported, attended by servants and apprentices. Nor did the king and his lords abandon such luxuries as silver plate and cutlery, princely beds, and wardrobes of furs and silks. Henry took his emblems of state, his chaplains, and their vestments and furnishings. On one wagon was packed a revered portion of 'the True Cross'.

Following the fall of Harfleur, the old and infirm among the townsfolk had been ejected to make room for the English, and the troops had been rewarded by a spell of authorized plundering.

Medieval torture –
the rack

146   Attack on a Normandy town (St James) showing scaling ladders and siege machines

Now discipline was reinforced. Henry's intention – to offer those in his path the choice between co-operation and safety on the one hand, resistance and devastation on the other – depended on being able to restrain his warriors.

The wisdom of this policy soon became evident. At Arques, approached on 11 October, and at Eu a day later, French garrisons not only gave him unimpeded passage in return for leaving the towns untouched but also provided his army with bread and wine. Elsewhere, some burning and sacking did take place. The chronicles speak of rape and sacrilege: 'The English made stables of the chapels; opened the coffers and stole the possessions of inhabitants; dragged women from the church and ravished them.' But hostile as well as amicable sources attest a new measure of control in the English ranks. One French writer actually portrays the troops of France as causing more terror among certain civilians than their enemies.

From Eu, Henry crossed the Bresle and set course for the Somme and Abbeville. A few miles from the river came a sudden halt. It was 13 October. In less than a week the expedition had completed more than half its planned itinerary. The health of most troops had much improved. Spirits were high. By evening, it could be expected that the Somme would be behind, pursuit forgotten.

The news that now reached the ranks produced a grim shock. The ford ahead was reported bristling with pointed stakes. On the far bank stood a French division at least the size of Henry's army. It was commanded by none other than Boucicaut.

That the renowned marshal could have overtaken the English was both bewildering and ominous. How far behind might the rest of the French army be? Where else on the Somme might Henry's men cross? To attempt to force the ford would be suicidal. Retreat towards Harfleur was unthinkable. At a council of crisis lasting two hours, the king and his captains were obliged to accept the only remaining course, namely to follow the south bank of the Somme inland in hope of finding an alternative crossing place.

The army turned upstream with foreboding. Every mile now placed Calais not nearer but farther off. The places by the wayside were unmentioned in Henry's plans: Pont Remy, Bailleul, Hangest, Pont de Metz, Boves. Everywhere, bridges had been destroyed or were defended by Boucicaut's men. The last of the food the troops had carried was eaten. There was little to be picked up. The populace had fled with its cattle and produce. All that remained in plenitude was wild nuts.

Morale plummeted. 'I who write and many others raised

bitterly anxious eyes to heaven imploring the mercy of the Almighty's celestial regard,' recorded a priest with the army. 'And we implored the glorious Virgin Mary and the blessed St George to mediate between God and our poor men.'

Fifty miles upstream of the ford it began to look as if the force would have to march another fifty, to the headwaters of the river, to reach the north bank. Discipline was threatened. Random burning and vandalism increased. At Boves, a supply of wine offered the troops escape from their misery. Many became drunk before Henry put a stop to the drinking.

Disorderliness among the footmen, who looked with growing envy at the horses of the knights, provoked the king to a harsh response. On 17 October, the day the army moved on, an offender was hanged from a tree and his comrades were made to march past the body.

The shadowing force on the north bank grew bolder. Crossing by bridge from the French-held town of Corbie, a party of knights charged amid the surprised English archers before they could draw their bows. Thereafter, every bowman carried a stout pointed stake by Henry's order. At the approach of enemy cavalry, the stakes were to be planted in the form of a crude fence, slanted at the horses' breasts.

Thus burdened, the weary troops plodded on. Reports that a great French army was advancing from the Seine increased English fears. The population no longer fled, but glared at the fugitives defiantly. A new mood of revenge swept the kingdom.

On the Seine, Henry's departure from Harfleur had galvanized the French lords. His small force seemed a tempting prize. Suddenly the Duke of Orleans joined the royal army with his fighting men. The Dukes of Bourbon, Berry, Bar and Alençon gave their full support. The Duke of Brittany arrived with a large force. Though the Duke of Burgundy still refused to stir himself, he allowed his brothers, Anthony Duke of Brabant and Philip Count of Nevers, to march to swell the royal host. In council at Rouen, the French nobles voted overwhelmingly for an immediate pursuit and confrontation of the enemy.

Charles's army had attained the remarkable strength of about 60,000 men. Many were poorly armed peasants and opportunistic vagabonds, but in men-at-arms alone – a muster of perhaps 15,000 – the French outnumbered the entire English force by almost three to one. The host attracted by its sheer size. Shopkeepers and artisans, including trained militia bowmen, flocked

to swell the numbers. So ample were the ranks that an offer by the citizens of Paris to provide 6,000 soldiers was turned down.

On the tactful advice of the veteran Duke of Berry, the unstable Charles and his son were persuaded to stay behind. The army headed for the Somme under three commands. Boucicaut and Albret, the supremo, went ahead with advanced guards; Orleans and Bourbon led the main force which followed them. How Boucicaut came to beat Henry to the Somme remains a mystery, but one of two answers is possible. Either he set out first having heard of the English plan, or he led an exclusively mounted force. At all events, his achievement was a brilliant stroke.

By 13 October Albret, advancing scarcely less rapidly, had also crossed the river, seemingly upstream of Boucicaut. At about the same time, the main body of the French army left Rouen, aiming to traverse the Somme at Amiens. Reaching the town a couple of days after Henry passed on the south bank, Bourbon and Orleans gained the north bank, turned east and followed Albret and Boucicaut upstream. The whole French army was now strung out behind the English king, its vanguard abreast of the foe across the water. Only by somehow stealing a march could Henry hope to cross the river unopposed.

On the morning of 18 October, he ventured to do this. Beyond Corbie the stream of the river coiled away to the English left in a broad sweep to Péronne before bending back toward the fords of Béthencourt and Voyennes. For north-bank traffic it meant a haul round the wide arc. Henry, on the other hand, was able to gain upwards of ten miles by marching along the base of the salient. That evening, he approached Béthencourt to find a crossing for the first time unguarded. True, the banks were marshy and the causeways demolished, but by filling the gaps with debris the troops at length reached the vital fords.

The passage began on the 19th. It was a tense operation. At any moment the French vanguard might have approached. Wagons lurched forwards and the animals lost their footing. Henry stood by, roaring encouragement. An hour after sunset, the last man splashed ashore on the far bank. A hundred miles to the north-west lay Calais, but the troops were too weary to contemplate further toil.

Next morning, a Sunday, they were still recovering when three French heralds arrived with a formal battle challenge. Livio describes the exchange in camp. The lords of France, said the heralds, had heard of Henry's intentions, 'and they inform thee by us that before thou comest to Calais they will meet with thee and be revenged of thy conduct'.

149

To which Henry, with courageous spirit and firm countenance, without anger or flush, replied calmly, 'Be all things according to the will of God.' When the heralds asked what road he would take, he answered, 'Straight to Calais, and if our enemies try to stop us it will be at their peril. We do not intend to seek them, but neither shall we go in fear of them ... We advise them not to disturb us, for the result must be a great effusion of Christian blood.'

The next four days were a nightmare for the English troops. The weather had broken. Rain squalls lashed their faces and drenched their clothes as, whatever Henry's fine words, they struggled grimly to outpace the French. Despite the conditions, they made as much as eighteen miles a day, spurred on by an awesome vision on the 21st.

Heading for Albert, the column came upon what a witness described as the 'strangely trodden' trail of an 'unimaginable host' – the churned wake of thousands of men and horses cutting the road diagonally from the Somme towards Baupaume. The French were still to the north, now united in full strength, an intimidating mass on the right flank. Fervently, the English chaplains prayed 'for God to have compassion upon us and, in his infinite goodness, to turn away from us the power of the French'. Less hopefully, Henry's knights had donned their armour and rode in constant fear of an attack.

On the 22nd and 23rd, the force toiled from Albert to Frévent, fifty miles or so short of Calais, while the enemy, marching for St Pol, drew so close that Henry's outriders could hear the music and babble of their cavalcade. Finally, on 24 October, the French streamed across the English path.

Having marched twelve miles from Frévent, the fugitives passed the small village of Blangy, in the valley of the Ternoise, and were mounting the far ridge, when a scout raised the first alarm. 'Retreating with a trembling heart and with the utmost speed his horse would carry him to the Duke of York [then commanding the vanguard] he said breathlessly, "Quickly be prepared for battle, as you are just about to fight against a world of innumerable people."'

Immediately ahead lay the village of Maisoncelles. From here the road to Calais ran north between the woods of Agincourt and Tramecourt, following a neck of clear land about half a mile wide, with some variation. Across the far end of this defile were arrayed upwards of 20,000 – 30,000 by some estimates – of the best troops in the French army. The dismay of the English force was complete.

In the next few hours, Henry tried hard to buy his way out, offering a high price in negotiation for the passage of his army. He was ready to suffer the humiliation of giving up Harfleur if the enemy commander would let him pass. But the French were not satisfied. They had Henry where they wanted him. He would have to fight.

The chroniclers make an elegant virtue of necessity. According to Livio, when Sir Walter Hungerford, one of the king's knights, protested the need for another 10,000 archers, Henry replied scornfully: 'Thou speakest foolishly, for by God, on whose grace I have relied, I would not, if I could, increase my number by one ... Dost thou not believe that the Almighty, with these his humble few, can vanquish such haughty opposition?'

Shakespeare made it a *happy* few, a 'band of brothers'. But if anything is certain, it is that Henry's troops were a far from happy band that cold, damp night in Maisoncelles on the eve of the feasts of St Crispin and St Crispinian.

The rival armies passed the night in very different moods. The English had marched for seventeen days under pressure, the last few in pouring rain. They were hungry, wet and bedraggled. Many were barefoot. Squatting on the soaked ground, Henry's men gazed into their camp fires and saw only defeat.

So quiet were the English lines that the French half suspected that their foes had slipped away in the dark. The Lord of St Remy, a Burgundian who had joined Henry, reported poetically that 'not a horse neighed'. Negotiations for safe conduct had broken down soon after dusk. There was no escape. Sombrely, the troops confessed to their priests and were shriven.

The French, too, had marched hard. Stripping the weaker elements from their army, the pace and fierce squalls had ensured that only the cream arrived at Agincourt. But for them excitement conquered weariness. The atmosphere in their lines was almost festive. Huge fires blazed. Nobles bawled at grooms and servants. Varlets hastened to lay clean straw on the ground where their masters sat. Knights diced for the prisoners they hoped to take. The clamour, likened by one chronicler to that of a country fair, could be heard in the English camp more than half a mile away.

At first light, on 25 October, the forces moved to battle stations. By chivalric requirements, the rectangular clearing flanked by the woods of Agincourt and Tramecourt presented an ideal field of contest. There were no hills, gulleys or hedges; simply a flat arena, in which the armies could meet head-on without distraction.

The English filled the southern or Maisoncelies end of the passage, about 950 yards wide, with three divisions abreast. Divisional conformation appears to have been conventional: men-at-arms flanked by forward-inclined wings of archers, thus presenting a point of archers between central and outer formations, with an oblique arm of bowmen at each shoulder of the army.

In one respect the customary disposition was modified. Archers constituted an uncommon proportion of Henry's force of about 5,500 troops, no more than perhaps 900 being men-at-arms. Consequently, while the armoured groups occupied less than a normal share of the front, the missile formations on the flanks were abnormally extended. Never before in the war had an army relied so heavily on its common ranks, men without chivalric pretension.

Henry might ride forth amid his knights on a grey palfrey, his surcoat resplendent, his helmet encircled by a crown set with precious stones, but his fate depended on the sons of cottagers and labourers, a tatterdemalion band of uncouth warriors who had lived in the past weeks scarcely better than animals. So sick were many of their sodden, louse-ridden garments that they had thrown them off and strapped their arrow-belts on naked flesh.

By contrast, the major element in the French force was its splendidly attired chivalry and stoutly armoured men-at-arms. So profuse was the nobility of France at Agincourt that there seemed to one observer more standards in a single line of Albret's host than there were lances in all Henry's army.

Aptly, since they outnumbered the English by at least four to one, the French occupied the wider end of the field, where the screening woods drew back slightly to give a front of three quarters of a mile, or thereabouts. Still, it was little enough space in which to deploy all the men involved, and the array necessarily ran into some depth.

Three divisions of French men-at-arms were set one behind the other, each spanning the defile and five or six men deep. The rear division was mounted; the knights in the other two deployed on foot. Crossbowmen appear to have been slotted between the leading divisions, while separate bodies of cavalry hovered on either wing. There were also a few cannons somewhere in the array, but the mass of troops around them rendered them useless.

Indeed, such was the jostling, rivalry and general lack of constraint in Albret's army that formal disposition was short-lived. 'All the lords wished to be in the first battalion,' wrote a French chronicler, 'for each was so jealous of the others that they could in no other way be reconciled'. Apart from Albret himself, such ostensible divisional leaders as Boucicaut and the Dukes of Bourbon and Orleans all insisted on a place in the front line, together with a bevy of counts and their formidable retinues.

Once there, they were content for the moment to await events. To this extent, the shrewder school of French military philosophy represented by Albret and Boucicaut appears to have prevailed over the premature chivalric reaction of Crécy and Poitiers. There was no hurry. The English could not get away.

For four hours the two armies faced each other across the field, neither making an offensive move. Tauntingly, as it must have seemed to their starved foes, groups of French knights sat under their banners eating and drinking. Others called to friends, or chatted with neighbours. It was not a development Henry could have relished. As an English eyewitness put it: 'The soldiers were much wearied with hunger, diseases and marching ... The longer they remained there the more they suffered the effects of exhaustion and debility.'

Periodically, Henry harangued his troops with stirring speeches, rousing their blood with gruesome hints of what the French would do to those they took alive. Priests perambulated the front line calling on God to enfeeble the enemy. But the waiting could not be allowed to last. Against all precepts, the weaker force would have to advance on the stronger.

153

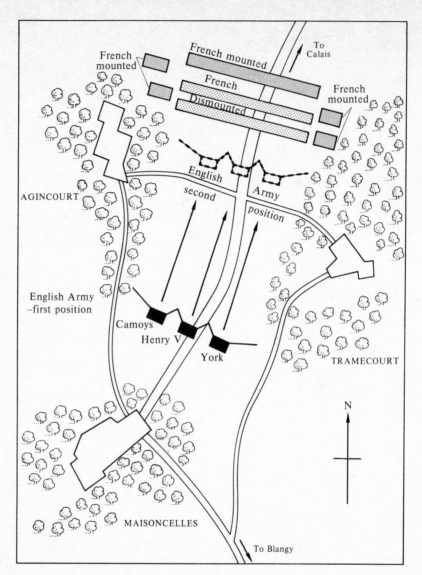

French mounted

French mounted

To Calais

French mounted

French

Dismounted

French mounted

AGINCOURT

English second Army position

English Army –first position

Camoys

Henry V

York

TRAMECOURT

N

MAISONCELLES

To Blangy

Battle of Agincourt

It was about 11 a.m. when the order finally rang out. Following tradition, each man in the English array knelt, made a cross on the ground and kissed it, taking a lump of soil in his teeth. Then the whole formation moved forward to shouts of 'Jesus, Mary and St George!'

Every warrior, including Henry, was now on foot. The king led the centre division; York the right. Lord Camoys, an experienced captain, took the left command. At extreme bowshot range, the line halted, the English archers placed arrows to greased string and 'the air was darkened by piercing shafts'.

154

Albret's tactics of controlled response demanded a missile counter, but three factors precluded this. In the first place, it is doubtful if the French bowmen were as numerous as their English counterparts. In the second place, had they been, the disadvantages of the crossbow would have ensured inferior firepower. Lastly, the crush of chivalry at the French front, squeezing lesser mortals rearwards, seriously restricted projectile operation.

With no chance of winning a missile duel, Albret was obliged to countenance direct attack. In any case, the French lords, provoked by hissing clothyards and the temptingly sparse ranks of the foe at close proximity, could no longer be held back. While the cavalry groups on the wings launched themselves at the offending English archers, the great mass of dismounted French knights lurched into motion, banners waving, trumpets blaring.

The horsemen met a sharp rebuff. At last, the pointed stakes cut at Corbie proved their value. Rammed into the soft soil ahead of the archers, they formed a rude but telling barrier against the few mounted knights who managed to get so far. These, charging head-down to protect their eyes from flying arrows, were pitched from impaled mounts among the bowmen and swiftly battered to oblivion. The remainder careered wildly into their dismounted compatriots, 'for their horses were so wounded by the arrows that they were unmanageable'.

Disconcerted by missiles and agonized animals, the dense contingents of pedestrian men-at-arms thrust with swelling anger towards the static English line. Where hooves had churned up the wet field, earth adhered and balled on tightly encased feet, adding to the burden of the French knights. Imperceptibly, the narrowing of the defile was increasing their compression. Further, determination to close with the English chivalry rather than the lower orders on the flanks exacerbated congestion in the French ranks.

There is no doubt that by the time they came up to Henry's front, Albret's formations were too tightly packed to fight efficiently. The authorities are unanimous. Many Frenchmen had not even the room to raise their sword arms. Struggling for space before the impact, they were barged forward by those behind. Some over-balanced. Unable to rise again, they were hacked to death by the English knights confronting them.

Others, unable to tug off their enclosing helmets, suffocated as their comrades tumbled on top of them. According to the chronicle of John Hardyng, who was present at Agincourt, more Frenchmen died in the mêlée 'through press than our own men could have slain'.

That is as maybe. Unquestionably, the vulnerability of Albret's overcrowded chivalry was exploited savagely by the English who, to all intents, found their prayers dramatically answered. Glimpsing reprieve from a fate that had seemed inescapable, the English knights lunged and chopped at their opponents with frenzied strength. In minutes, hundreds of Frenchmen had fallen.

Observing the French disorder, the English archers now seized the initiative. Grabbing such weapons as the foe had dropped in confusion, these deprived and unprepossessing warriors 'sallied out upon them and, hastening where there were breaches, killed and disabled the French ... and met with little or no resistance. And the English, cutting right and left, pushed on ... with the King of England in person.'

Incredibly, the battle was won within half an hour. In that space, both main French foot formations had been committed and defeated while the remaining cavalry, deterred by mounds of their own dead and the elated visage of the English, had begun to melt from the bloody field.

Within the bounds of possibility, the French knights engaged had fought valiantly. But, surrounded by confusion, and immobilized by their armour and the rapidly worsening mud, they fell easy victims to the sanguinary and agile English bowmen. 156 Albret himself, and the Dukes of Alençon, Brabant and Bar, were killed; Orleans, Bourbon and Boucicaut were captured. On the other side, the Duke of York was dead, suffocated as he sprawled on the ground, too encumbered and portly to raise himself. Gloucester had been wounded by a thrust beneath his breast plate, but was dragged to safety after Henry, his brother, had stood guard over his prone form.

By midday, the English army had largely diverted its efforts from fighting to seeking prisoners worth ransoming. The piles of dead were turned over; the living sorted from the corpses; helmets prised open and armour unriveted. Gradually, those who could walk were marshalled by their captors.

While this proceeded, what remained of the French cavalry chafed at a distance. Two nobles, the Counts of Marle and Fauquemberghes, had gathered 600 men-at-arms and showed signs of attempting a new attack. Already, a mob of French peasants had plundered Henry's baggage while his army was preoccupied. The men could not hold their prisoners and resist assault at the same time. Ensuring that his personal captives, the great French captains, were made safe, the king peremptorily ordered that the rest should be put to death.

The order was backed, in view of its unpopularity, by a promise to hang any Englishman who disobeyed. Countless prisoners were butchered, 'killed in cold blood and cut in pieces, heads and faces, which was a fearful sight to see', averred a witness. Though the slaughter was halted when the French threat proved a false alarm, some sources say the victims were more numerous than the actual battle casualties.

The true losses on either side are unknown, but dependable estimates show the huge disparity. Modern historians put the French dead at Agincourt between 8,000 and 10,000, including almost 100 lords and 1,500 lesser noblemen. When the local churchyards could hold no more bodies, 5,800 remained to be thrown into great pits.

Against this devastating toll, this huge forfeit of French chivalry, the modesty of Henry's losses was astonishing. At the outside, English casualties have been numbered at 500; more reliably, at a quarter of that number. And the bulk of these were not mortally wounded.

Most of the English dead were placed in a barn near Maison-celles and cremated by the firing of the building, which blazed all night. A few bodies, including that of the Duke of York, were deemed too important for such an end. They were boiled and their bones extracted for conveyance home.

Chapter 9

After Monmouth

Agincourt, the last great pitched battle of the Hundred Years War between representative armies of the French and English kingdoms, closed the chapter of warfare opened at Crécy. If Poitiers had demonstrated the reluctance of a military caste to learn from experience, the new French upset was a lesson impossible to ignore.

The days of French chivalry were numbered. Socially, its decadence was increasingly emphasized by writers such as Juvénal and Meschinot. Militarily, it had suffered a stunning blow, not only in the letting of its life blood at Agincourt but in the humiliation of defeat by an army composed largely of vulgar bowmen.

Outstandingly, Agincourt proclaimed the hour of the common soldier. Skill and valour, acknowledged the French author and diplomat Alain Chartier, were not exclusive to the knightly class. Soldiers of lowly birth might achieve greater renown than the sons of counts. It was a thought to be pondered by Frenchmen, not least the citizen volunteers rejected before the battle by their warlords. The beginnings of patriotism were astir in France, but the people lacked inspiring leadership.

In England, the same dawning of national sentiment responded to victory. Not only in London, where Henry's return via Calais was the occasion for popular rejoicing on a massive scale, but through much of the country, the exploits of the men of Agincourt excited Englishmen. Henry's plan for the systematic conquest of France could now go ahead.

For a while, organized resistance was minimal. The French king was demented. The Orleanist faction had very nearly been annihilated at Agincourt. The Burgundians still held aloof from war with England. Nursing its injuries, the rest of the nobility was not encouraged by the dauphin's nominal chieftainship.

Though sieges were plentiful, Normandy fell without a battle. Worse, for Henry's enemies, in 1419 the dauphin senselessly murdered John of Burgundy and the Burgundian faction joined forces with the English. From now on, French armies faced Anglo–French armies on the battlefield. The war increasingly devolved on French politics. Within two years, Henry's death produced the crucial watershed.

Opposite Joan of Arc presented to Charles VII of France

In 1422, having begun the arduous task of reducing in detail those provinces where his title was still denied, the English king contracted fever at Meaux. He died in August. Two months later, Charles VI drew his last breath, leaving the crown of France contested by the dauphin and Henry VI of England, a mere infant.

Morale in the dauphinist camp received a powerful boost.
Under a new constable, Bernard of Armagnac, the Orleanist
party was reviving. Its opponents could derive little cheer from a
monarch in the cradle. Above all, the Anglo–Burgundian cause
had lost its driving genius.

For all his misdirected ambition and unlikeable attributes,
Henry of Monmouth had provided uncommon military leadership. By a combination of discipline and infectious fervour, he had
imbued his armies with a conviction of their superiority which even
their enemies had come to share. Without him, the unnatural
fabric of Anglo–French union had to crumble.

Had the dauphinists possessed a general of merit, it must have
happened rapidly. But they did not. Of a less than brilliant selection
between the camps, John, Duke of Bedford and uncle to the infant
king, proved the best man. So the wearing struggle dragged on.

At Cravant in August 1423, and Verneuil in August 1424,
Anglo–Burgundian armies won decisive victories, though with
significantly less ease than had Henry at Agincourt. French captains
were learning. Whether fighting with Bedford on the one side, or
with a pro-dauphinist Scottish contingent on the other, they
160   displayed less impetuosity and more forethought than hitherto.

Indeed, at Cravant the dauphin's army, though superior in numbers, adopted a defensive posture in the field. Its undoing was mediocre generalship and the better integration of the rival force.

Bedford's lieutenant, the Earl of Salisbury, had taken pains to form 'one indivisible army' of English and Burgundians. According to the chronicler John de Waurin, who probably was present, the soldiers of each contingent were encouraged to mix harmoniously, and marched to battle 'with brotherly affection'. By contrast, the French and Scots in the opposing camp seldom got on well, and fought without close co-operation. Before Verneuil, the dauphinist commander, the Count of Aumâle, engaged in raging controversy with the captains of his Scottish allies, thereafter exerting little influence over them.

The battle has been misrepresented as 'a second Agincourt'. Certainly Bedford's army took the field in formations abreast, archers on the wings, advancing to missile range while the enemy attacked with cavalry on the flanks. But these were conventions of the period. The force facing Bedford contained a lower proportion of chivalry, more general troops and, despite its uninspiring leader, better captains than the French army at Agincourt. Moreover, the actions of individual groups, while wrecked by the precipitate retreat of Aumâle himself, were resourceful and effective.

Bedford's archers, attacked before they could embed their stakes, were swept from his right wing. A penetrating thrust to his rear caused confusion in that area. Part of his force withdrew in panic. According to one report, a Captain Young was later charged and hanged for leading 500 men from the field. But the reformation of French fighting capacity was yet to come.

In 1428 Bedford reached the Loire to besiege Orleans. He was over-extended, the tide turning. Camped beneath the walls of a well garrisoned and fortified city, his army was absurdly small.

By now, northern France was sick of English domination and factional squabbling. Weary of the vendettas and vices of noblemen, the people were beginning to forget themselves as Orleanists and Burgundians; to discover that, after all, they were Frenchmen. Chartier's writing, asserting the martial potential of common men, implied self-help. But if the people were to recover they had to find faith and hope, the inspirational guidance they had so far lacked. The stage was set. It needed only an actor to play the role.

As a militarist, Joan of Arc was poorly qualified. She knew little more of the science of war, so far as it existed, than might have been expected of a country girl. But as a symbol of the spirit of outraged France, she was superbly cast.

Of Champagne descent, her family were well-to-do farmers
uprooted by the shift of war. The mystic visions she claimed might
not have impressed later governments, but at a time when prophets
and seers abounded in the councils of powerful men the Maid's
insistence on superhuman motivation was not dismissed. It was
her profound belief that she was to be instrumental in evicting
the English.

The dauphin, beguiled by Joan's assurance that his enthrone-
ment at Reims would soon follow, thought her worthy of probation.
Accordingly, in spring 1429, the young woman was allowed to
accompany the Duke of Alençon, himself a youthful prince, with
an army of 4,000 to the relief of Orleans.

Whatever the men thought of her, she made her presence felt.
Swearing was prohibited, prostitutes were driven off, mass and
confessions became obligatory for the troops. If such provisions
were remarkably akin to those of Henry V, the broader appeal of
Joan was quite unique. Entering Orleans ahead of the main
relieving army late in April, she quickly enheartened the occupants.

The situation was made for Joan's talents. Six months of siege
had left the citizens demoralized, fearful of treachery in their
midst. In fact, their besiegers were as badly off. Inferior in number

to Alençon's force, beset by sickness and desertion, Bedford was incapable of maintaining a close blockade. With spirit, the communal militia might have chased him off. Joan provided the confidence. In a series of dashing sorties from the city, the English posts were demolished and the siege raised. Surprised and elated by their own strength, the French swept one after another of the enemy's garrisons from the Loire.

On 19 June an Anglo–French army of reinforcement under the Earl of Shrewsbury, Lord Talbot, was routed in a matter of minutes at Patay. Alençon and a fellow commander, the Count of Dunois, had burst upon it with their eager troops before it could form up to meet the charge. For the English, it was a novel experience. Since Agincourt, their foes had approached with hesitation. Now they were transformed.

The legend of Joan was born. The dauphin gave her the credit for Patay, though she had not arrived until the action was over. She was pictured commanding French forces, though her role was advisory not executive. The Maid exhorted the soldiers and gave captains the recommendations of her 'voices'. But the captains led the companies and made the decisions, frequently against Joan's counsel. There is no evidence that she worried anybody in the English camp.

All the same, her influence flourished. Frenchmen were inspired by the strange girl who dressed as a warrior. French arms commanded new respect. In July, when Joan accompanied the dauphin to Reims for his promised coronation, neither English nor Burgundians halted them. The march was a military promenade.

From Reims, the newly anointed Charles VII asserted sway over Laon, entered Soissons and advanced to Brie. Now it was the foe who was hesitant. No longer did English troops expect to fight outnumbered and triumph. Everywhere, submissions and protestations of loyalty met the French king. Senlis, in Valois, surrendered. Compiègne was captured. Confidently, Charles marched on Paris, whose pro-Burgundian burgesses still controlled the city. Joan went with him.

The campaign was a failure. Joan advised the forcing of the bastions by escalade, but the royal army lacked adequate equipment, and Charles should have ignored her. The assault, in September, miscarried. Joan's star had begun to wane.

Next year, 1430, the king remained to the south, short of money. Joan joined the loyalist bands which continued to operate in the north, but her presence did not bring them much luck. At last,

Joan of Arc leading
troops at Orleans: a
romantic interpretation

Charles's ministers and captains shifted from grudging tolerance of his unorthodox military adviser to open hostility.

Among a knighthood riddled with greed and self-interest, Joan's appeal to duty and self-sacrifice, not to say her influence with common troops, had always seemed malignant. To the clergy, her usurpation of ecclesiastic prerogatives was as great a threat. There was little gloom in established circles when she was captured by Burgundians near Compiègne and sold to Bedford. In May 1431, Joan of Arc was burned as a heretic at Rouen after trial by French clerics of the opposing faction.

By now, the northern insurrection, though prolonged, was irreversible. The key factor was the gradual desertion of the English alliance by the Burgundians. Philip of Burgundy made terms with his father's murderer in 1435. The following year, the burgher militia of Paris refused to oppose Charles's army, and the small English garrison surrendered there. Bedford's death spared him the dismal news.

Had the French king possessed more vigour and wealth, the fall of Paris must have heralded the speedy reclamation of all France. But his resources were low, his realm exhausted. On the other side,

Joan of Arc approaching Chinon: an early tapestry

165

an English government which might still have made peace to advantage clung to outdated hopes. Stubborn pride kept the war alive.

Like France, England could spare few men and little money for the contest. Yet somehow, largely due to the tireless efforts of its veteran commanders, the Earls of Shrewsbury and Warwick, the English cause survived, even flickered spasmodically with success. From Rouen, Shrewsbury persistently launched his meagre forces against the enemy, once sallying on Paris itself across a frozen Seine.

Between 1444 and 1448, a truce made possible by the appearance of an English peace party led by the Earl of Suffolk was accompanied by a diminution of Henry's claims and the young king's marriage to the French princess Margaret of Anjou. The year 1449 saw a resumption of fighting, but this time the end was near.

French arms were now ascendant both numerically and technically. The feudal element had practically disappeared. In its place was a professional force of mounted troops and bowmen, backed by paid militia, whose strength in really effective soldiers was formidable: perhaps 30,000 men available to campaign in Normandy, half infantry, half cavalry. In addition, there was a powerful train of siege guns and lighter cannons, built up over a period by an artillery enthusiast named John Bureau, one of two brothers with financial posts in the French government.

Since the English had no field army in Normandy, their neglected force being wholly dispersed in scattered garrisons, the action proceeded as a succession of sieges: in effect, a reversal of Henry V's conquest. Most were promptly terminated by Bureau's guns. Castle after castle surrendered or was blown to pieces. Henry would have marvelled at the ease with which the French artillery disposed of Harfleur and, soon afterwards, Honfleur.

By 1450, the remnants of the English army of occupation were beleaguered under an incapable governor, the Duke of Somerset, in the area around Caen and Bayeux. At this point, the English government, having sent neither supplies nor reinforcements to the duchy in twelve months, awakened to the crisis. A scratch army was raised and the best commander available, Sir Thomas Kyriel, a long-serving soldier, placed in charge. In March it sailed from Portsmouth, 2,500 strong, and landed at Cherbourg. It was to be the last army to cross the Channel during the Hundred Years War.

Kyriel's objective was the relief of Bayeux. With the addition of 1,800 men scraped together for him by Somerset, he paused to recover Valognes, in the Cotentin, then crossed the Vire and

Henry VI invests John
Talbot with the sword
of office as Constable
of France, 1442

advanced into Bessin. Apart from the main French army, then
approaching Caen from the west, two smaller enemy forces were
in the duchy.

On the afternoon of 15 April, one of these, commanded by the
Count of Clermont, a son of the Duke of Bourbon, made contact
with Kyriel at Formigny, ten miles short of Bayeux. The ensuing
battle, though small in scale, was of high tactical import.

Kyriel stationed his army, now rather less than 4,000 strong,
across the Bayeux road amid orchards and gardens in the region
of an ample brook. The formation was unexceptional. Dismounted
men-at-arms held the centre with archers angled forward in
flanking wings. As well as the customary screen of stakes, holes and
trenches had been prepared to obstruct charging horsemen.

Clermont, advancing by the road against the English front,
halted 'two bow-shots' from the enemy. With no more than 2,000
troops, his hope of overcoming Kyriel was based on a conjunction
with the second French force, slightly exceeding his own in
strength, led by Arthur of Richemont, Constable of France.
Richemont, a few miles to the English left, was in fact approaching
at the maximum possible speed – a rare example of battlefield
concentration by medieval armies operating on independent lines.

Meanwhile, Clermont preoccupied the English line. Pushing 167

168   Battle to capture a medieval town

culverins, or field guns, through his front ranks, he played round-shot on the enemy position until Kyriel's archers were goaded into charging the cannons. This development settled the issue. Deprived of missile cover and proper control of his army, Kyriel had no chance as Richemont came up on his left flank. Simultaneously, Clermont advanced. Caught between two enemy fronts and the brook of Formigny, the English were massacred.

About 500 archers fought to the death in an orchard at the brook-side. Kyriel himself was surrounded and captured. The fraction of his army that escaped was useless as a fighting force. Within a few weeks, Somerset had capitulated. The English administration of Normandy was over. Formigny slammed the door on Lancastrian ambitions in France with a bang – the literal bang of cannonry.

Potentially, the English kingdom remained formidable, charged by the epic performance of Henry V and the sheer audacity of more than a century of offensive war against its larger neighbour. In the course of the struggle, Englishmen had become aware of a national strength, an economic independence unknown to earlier generations. But the line had to be drawn at last. In the end, the people had been subjected to costs they refused to bear.

The glory of the final hour belonged to France – yet the glory was ephemeral. Beneath it lay an exhaustion far deeper than England's. For the French kingdom, a hundred years of war on its own soil, repeated devastation and impoverishment, had been an immense ordeal. Centuries would pass before the realm resumed its former position in the affairs of Europe.

Militarily, radical changes had come to pass. Among others, the years of conflict had embraced the decline of feudal cavalry, the replacement of chivalric by professional attitudes, the rise of patriotic motivation, the tactical development of long-range hand weapons, and, finally, the first instances of general actions decided by artillery.

Three years after Formigny, the last of Henry V's generals, John Talbot, Earl of Shrewsbury, arrived in Bordeaux in a bid to prevent Guienne going the way of Normandy. Raising every Englishman and Gascon he could muster, he marched on the French at Castillon with a mighty column. Its vanguard was ripped to pieces by entrenched artillery; the old earl himself was felled by a roundshot.

Amid the gunsmoke of a new martial era, the last Anglo–Gascon army perished wholesale. Of all France, Calais alone remained to England. That was to remain the situation for another hundred years.

Select Bibliography

No attempt will be made here to list the mass of records, chronicles and other primary sources for the Hundred Years War. The following books are noted as an introduction to the further reading available in the general field.

For those concerned simply with the three great land battles and their campaigns, eminently readable expositions are to be found in *The Crécy War* by Lieutenant-Colonel Alfred H. Burne (London, 1955); *The Black Prince's Expedition 1355–57* by H. J. Hewitt (Manchester, 1958); and Christopher Hibbert's *Agincourt* (London, 1964). An outstanding summary of the period from a French viewpoint is provided by Professor Edouard Perroy in *The Hundred Years War* (London, 1962), while a series of fascinating essays on various aspects of the conflict is offered by eight distinguished historians in *The Hundred Years War*, edited by Kenneth Fowler (London, 1971).

Armitage-Smith, S., *John of Gaunt*, London, 1904.

Blair, Claude, *European Armour*, London, 1958.

Burne, Alfred H., *The Crécy War*, London, 1955.

Burne, Alfred H., *The Agincourt War*, London, 1956.

Chrimes, S. B., *English Constitutional Ideas in the 15th Century*, Cambridge, 1936.

Coulton, G. G., *The Black Death*, Cambridge, 1929.

Davies, J. D. Griffith, *Henry V*, London, 1935.

Fowler, K. (ed.), *The Hundred Years War*, London, 1971.

Hewitt, H. J., *The Black Prince's Expedition 1355–57*, Manchester, 1958.

Hibbert, Christopher, *Agincourt*, London, 1964.

Holmes, George, *The Later Middle Ages 1272–1485*, London, 1962.

Jacob, E. F., *Henry V and the Invasion of France*, London, 1947.

Lodge, E. C., *Gascony under English Rule*, London, 1926.

Lucas, H. S., *The Low Countries and the Hundred Years War*, London, 1929.

Mathew, G., *Ideals of Knighthood in Late Fourteenth-Century England* (in *Studies in Medieval History*), Oxford, 1948.

Myers, A. R., *England in the Later Middle Ages*, London, 1952.

Newhall, R. A., *The English Conquest of Normandy*, Newhaven, Conn., 1924.

Oman, C., *A History of the Art of War in the Middle Ages*, London, 1924.

Perroy, E., *The Hundred Years War*, London, 1951.

Power, E., *The Wool Trade in English Medieval History*, Oxford, 1941.

Powicke, Michael, *Military Obligation in Medieval England: A Study in Liberty and Duty*, Oxford, 1962.

Smail, R. C., *The Art of War*, Vol. 1 of *Medieval England* (ed. Austin Lane Poole), Oxford, 1958.

Steel, A., *Richard II*, Cambridge, 1940.

Thrupp, S. L., *The Merchant Class of London 1300–1500*, Chicago, 1948.

Unwin, G., *Finance and Trade under Edward III*, Manchester, 1918.

Vale, M. G. A., *English Gascony 1399–1453*, Oxford, 1970.

Index

Stratford, John, Archbishop, 45
Stratford, Robert, 45
Sudbury, Sir Simon, 124
Suffolk, Earl of: in Guienne *1355*, 70; Poitiers, 88; and Henry V, 133, 142, 166
Swynderby, William, 122

Talleyrand-Perigord, Cardinal de, 89
Tard-Venus, 106
Thiérache campaign, 33, 34, 103
Thomas of Woodstock, 116–117
Thomas (ship), 39, 120
Toulouse, 71, 74, 76, 77
Touraine, 68
Tournai: Edward III at, 42–3
Tours, 84

Trastamare, Henry of, 107, 114
Trebes, sack of, 75
Trinity Royal (flagship), 135
Tyler, Wat, 124–6

Umfraville, Sir Gilbert, 143

Valognes, 166; Treaty of, 79
Verneiul, 81, 160–61
Vernon, 142
Vienne, John of, 121
Vierzon, 83–4

Wales, 25; rebels, 129; troops from, 48
Walworth, William, 124

War of the Two Joans, 46–7
Warwick, Earl of, 70; at Poitiers, 88, 89, 91, 93; banished by Richard II, 126; *15c.*, 166
Waurin, John de, 161
Winchelsea, 119–20, 121
Woodland, standard-bearer, 97
wool, Edward III's negotiations re, 30–31, 32, 33–4, 43
Wycliffe, John, 122, 126

York, Duke of, in France with Henry V, 133, 143, 150, 154, 157
Yorkshire, 124
Young, Captain, hanged, 161

Zweibrücken, Count of, 32